S O F T   S K I I N G

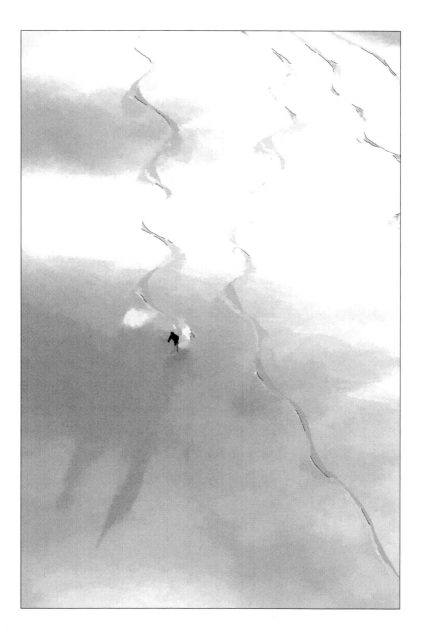

SOFT SKIING

THE SECRETS OF EFFORTLESS,

LOW-IMPACT SKIING

FOR OLDER SKIERS

LITO TEJADA-FLORES

WESTERN EYE PRESS

FIRST EDITION

WINTER

2010

This book is published by Western Eye Press, a small independent publisher (very small, and very independent) with a home base in the Colorado Rockies and an office in Sedona Arizona, using an innovative on-demand publishing system.

Western Eye Press
P O Box 1008
Sedona, Arizona 86339
1 800 333 5178
www.WesternEyePress.com
First edition, winter 2010.
ISBN 978-0-941283-22-9
Cover photos & most of the photo-illustrations
by Linde Waidhofer.
Designed by the author in InDesign CS3.
The text is set in Galliard roman.
The display type is Hypatia Pro.

CONTENTS

Skiing has always represented a kind of liberation from gravity, from weight, from the slow-speed limits of everyday reality.

INTRODUCTION

This is a book that I never thought I would write. Why not? Because, like you perhaps, I never even imagined I might grow old—older yes, but never old. Seems there is more than a little Peter Pan in all of us. But here I am, 68 and counting, and more importantly, 68 and still skiing, skiing with abandon. Skiing I tell myself, and my friends all agree, better than ever. My gray-white hair and gray-white beard haven't slowed me down, and even a broken back (don't ask, but it wasn't a skiing accident) a few years ago only slowed me down a little, and just for one season.

Nowadays, when I hit the slopes, I confess that I am more amazed and delighted than ever at the ease with which I can ski, at this effortless sensation of flying. Skiing has always represented a kind of liberation from gravity, from weight, from the slow-speed limits of everyday reality. But now, now that I have spent most of my life on skis, I realize that it has also become a liberation from the slowly accumulating insults of passing years. It's true. Like you, I was stronger and faster in my twenties than I am today. As a young rock climber, then a young skier, I never had to "get in shape." I just stayed in shape. Nowadays it takes some doing. That doing, to be sure, is still fun. I am lucky enough to live in the foothills of the Rockies in Colorado, and my daily summer walks up the canyons above our house, with my indefatigable golden dog seem less like an exercise regime than an ongoing although low-key mountain adventure.

I hike, I ski. The two are not, it turns out, unrelated. And the subtext of this book—my message to older skiers, and to would-be skiers of all ages—is simple: if you can walk, you can ski. Gracefully, efficiently, elegantly. And you should.

Skiing is a wonderful and altogether crazy sport. And I am hardly the first person to say that, or think that. The wonderful aspects of sliding down a snowy mountainside on skis are legion. All skiers have their own personal catalog of great moments, pure delight, poetry in motion... But the crazy part? It seems to me totally unexpected, and not entirely logical that skiing is a sport at which one can not only excel, but get better and better as the years go by. Most sports put a great premium on youth, most athletes peak somewhere around their twenties, and then it's all downhill. A tale of reduced performance and fading memories. But not skiing. Yes, of course, competitive skiing actually does fit that pattern. Champions and would-be champions are young, explosively strong, and follow a regime of training and competing that would exhaust older skiers. But skiing is so much more than ski racing...

Skiing is making first tracks in a foot of fresh powder. Skiing is playing follow-the-leader through a forest of widely spaced trees. Skiing is cruising down freshly groomed slopes that go on and on and on.... Skiing is that last run of the day watching the evening clouds turn pink above frosted trees. Skiing is feeling so comfortable on those two slippery boards that you realize you can enjoy the view while you ski, or whistle a tune, or admire the graceful form of your skiing companions. No stress, no crisis, no winners, no losers. Just the pure pleasure of pure motion through space.

How is this possible? Why is the possible? Two reasons: First, skiing is mostly a sport of borrowed forces. Expert skiers are seldom called upon to use their own muscular force to make something happen. Gravity is the motor. A great motor. Pulling us down a long inclined plane. A motor that never wears out, never stops, is always there when the skier says: *Now*.

And the second reason is the phenomenal, and continuous improvement in the gear we use to ski. Skiing depends on stuff, on equipment. You can't ski without skis. And that's only the beginning. Skis, boots, poles, bindings… And all of them, today, so different, so much better than what we skied with ten years ago, five years ago. And there is no end in sight.

I used to have a sort of Platonic vision of the ideal ski turn, a picture in my mind's eye, or perhaps a moving image on my mind's video screen, of a wonderful pure carved turn. I could see it, but I could never quite do it. Today, that perfect turn is easy—not because I got better, but because my skis and boots are so much better. Those great turns are somehow built into our modern gear, waiting for us. And my job, in this book will be in large part showing you just how to access them.…

In this short introduction I want to paint a picture of skiing as a sport not just of graceful movement, but of easy, almost effortless movement. Yet I know this image does not hold true for all skiers. A lot of skiers, far too many skiers actually, struggle and sweat getting down the mountain. A lot of skiers feel that this sport is a kind of three-way wrestling match between them and their skis and the mountain. Even after years of skiing, these skiers still don't feel like experts, and indeed they aren't. When an expert skier swoops gracefully by them, they ruefully imagine that what that skier is doing, although it looks easy, must be quite difficult, much harder than what they are doing to control and guide their skis. Wrong.

My life and work as a ski teacher has been focused on showing that this need not be the case. Expert skiing is actually *much easier* than what most intermediate skiers or "average skiers" go through to get from the top of the mountain to the bottom. Expert skiing can be, and should be, almost effortless. And this is especially important for skiers who are no longer young, who no longer have the energy to wrestle with their skis. Sound good? Of course it does. In this book I'm going to show you how.

But let me underline something before we start. In this book, I am not talking about a special flavor of skiing, fine-tuned exclusively for older skiers. The moves, the techniques, the learning patterns I am going to share with you in this book, are all about classical mainstream expert skiing. So what then is different? Why did I bother to write *Soft Skiing*? Why are you going to bother reading it? It's all a matter of emphasis, of a different focus. From a technical point of view, much of what I am about to present in this book can also be found in my earlier book, *Breakthrough on the New Skis*. But this time,

I'm approaching the same moves, the same turns, with a special focus on ease, comfort and efficiency. Instead of covering the whole range of modern expert skiing, I'll spend my time (and your time too) working on techniques that save energy, that make skiing more graceful, and flat-out physically easier. That's the way I ski. And if you were intrigued by the promise of this book's title, I think that's the way you will enjoy skiing. *Soft Skiing* has turned into a very personal book for me, So in Part I, instead of diving headfirst into a practical ski lesson, I am going to start by sharing the story of how I discovered the tricks and delights of soft skiing. I hope your journey will be as enjoyable as mine has been.

It was Switzerland. It was late autumn and snow was creeping down the slopes of the peaks above town....

Part I

MY STORY
HOW I FELL INTO SOFT SKIING

Learning to ski.

I'd better begin at the beginning.

It was Switzerland. It was late autumn and snow was creeping down the slopes of the peaks above town – the little town of Leysin in the French-speaking canton of Vaud. Winter was almost upon us and I was desperate to learn to ski... Or, if not desperate, at least a bit anxious about it. Why? Because a good rock-climbing friend (I was a fanatical rock climber and mountaineer in those days) had just gotten me a job as a sports teacher and dormitory proctor at a private American High School, high in the French speaking Swiss Alps. A wonderful way to spend the winter in the Alps after a summer of exciting climbs around Chamonix and Mont Blanc. There was only one problem. Being a sports teacher for the Leysin American School meant that I would be spending most of the coming winter on skis, teaching skiing to the school's teenage students. And I didn't know how to ski. "Don't worry, Lito," my friend Royal Robbins had told me, "you can start out with the beginners and just stay one step ahead of them." (Gulp.)

Royal Robbins, one of America's leading rock climbers, had also spent his summer in the Alps climbing, but unlike me, Royal was already a certified ski instructor with years of ski teaching behind him at Sugar Bowl in the California Sierras. And this experience had landed him the job of sports director at the Leysin private school. Royal loaned me his ski teacher's manual from Sugar Bowl, told me to read it, and assured me that everything would work out as soon as the snow arrived. I wasn't so sure. Autumn was turning the larch needles yellow. The shops of our cobble-stoned village high above the Rhone valley were full of new ski equipment, bright new ski sweaters and parkas. It was another world. What was I doing there?

While I supervised soccer matches and taught the kids rock climbing, I hatched a secret plan. I had already bought my first skis and boots. Whenever I had a free hour or two, I would throw my boots in my pack, put my skis over my shoulder and start hiking, up to the top of the mountain where the snow was already starting to accumulate even though the snow line hadn't reached our village below. Near the top of the *Solacyre* or *la Berneuse*, our two local ski mountains, I would put on my gear, start side-stepping up and down a short hill to pack out a practice slope. Patiently, starting with page one, I began to practice all the moves and maneuvers described in Royal's circa-1960s ski-instruction book. It was the very first ever American ski-instructors' manual published by a relatively young organization called PSIA (Professional Ski Instructors of America). And my solitary practice sessions on top of the mountain sort of worked, up to a point....

It wasn't too hard. Soon I could snowplow, and then turn, and then skid a bit. Still there was this thing called a "parallel turn" that totally eluded me. I knew it was supposed to be a graceful move, a graceful experience. But it wasn't. When I tried it, after reading and re-reading the manual, I would usually "catch an edge" and crash, or at best, twist my skis awkwardly into a new direction, surviving each attempted turn with something like a sigh of relief mixed with exasperation. Parallel turns just weren't working. The ski season would soon be upon us and if those cynical expatriate American teenagers ever figured out that I was completely faking it, I knew I'd be toast. What to do? I needed a plan B.

Plan B appeared in our village bookstore in the form of a most interesting book with a very simple blue-and-white cover and a lot of equally simple line drawings of skiers making those elusive parallel turns, all kinds of parallel turns. The book was in French no less. The title was *Savoir Skier*, by someone I had never heard of named Georges Joubert. Luckily, I read French, and the book turned out to be a very good read. Even better, this book promised to deliver the secrets of modern skiing. And I guess it did, because it effectively changed my life.

There was a full moon over Leysin. In the far distance, off there across Lake Geneva, the sawtooth, snow-plastered peaks of Les Dents du Midi almost glowed in the night. The long smooth grassy slope just below our school building (which looked for all the world like a TB sanitarium from Thomas Mann's novel, *The*

Magic Mountain) was newly covered with a foot of fresh powder snow. It was almost midnight, most of the kids were sleeping or at any rate, pretending to sleep while up to other mischief. I had just finished reading Joubert's explanation of something he called *anticipation*, something that he promised would make parallel turns effortless. His idea was that that skiers could first turn their bodies to face down the hill, and then simply lean, or tilt in that direction, smoothly moving their bodies down the hill, and their skis would follow, unwinding easily, inevitably, beneath them into the turn. And then? That's all. Because, as Joubert assured his readers, skis are meant to turn. Once you start them into a turn, they will keep turning, on their own. No more need to twist them around.

Could Joubert be right? Or was it just the elegance of the French language, or the lateness of the hour that made me want to believe him? I couldn't wait to try this *anticipation* thing, and I didn't. A little before midnight there I was down in the bright moonlight on that smooth alp below the school. And it worked, worked like a charm. My skis wanted to turn, they seemed to turn on their own. My first real parallel turns. Easy parallel turns. Almost effortless. And Joubert was also right that all one needed to do was start those skis turning, and they would do the rest. They would keep on turning. What a wonderful feeling. What a revelation.

The next morning there were a lot of S shaped tracks down that snowy meadow below the school. And I knew I was going to survive my first winter in the Alps without being disgraced as a fake. I had learned three things. First, how to easily trigger a parallel turn. Second, that such a turn, once started, would keep going, on its own. And last but not least, that it was really possible to learn to ski from a book. That final discovery shaped a lot of what I've done since, and encouraged me, much later, to write my own ski books. Altogether it was a pretty romantic introduction—although I didn't fully understand it that memorable night in Leysin—to the whole notion of *soft skiing*. Doing more with less, on skis.

That first winter on skis passed awfully fast. Once the lifts opened I found myself giving ski lessons every afternoon, just as Royal promised, starting of course with the total beginners. And yes, I always managed to keep one step, or several, ahead of my young students who never figured out that I had just started skiing only a few weeks before they had. There were surprises and comic moments. I took my teaching responsibilities so seriously that I tried to think through everything that could possibly happen, or possibly go wrong, in a ski class. But I was unprepared for a cheerful roly-poly young freshman who was so stout that he literally could never get back on his feet once he fell over. (Removing his skis was the only solution). And in short order I was hooked, I spent all my free-time on the slopes, and aside from my afternoon classes I had a lot of free time. Skiing totally captured my attention, and my imagination. At night I would dream about skiing. In the morning I would be the first skier at the chair-lift across the street from school and spend all morning recreating those dreams, on real snow, with real turns, real runs, real wind in my face. It was a helluva good introduction to skiing.

There were frustrations too. Chief among them was deep, "bottomless" powder snow. That long-ago Leysin winter was a good snow year. Storms kept the mountain fresh, and since the lifts ran up above timberline, there was lots of space to make your own tracks in the periodic blankets of powder that covered the Vaudoise Alps. If only I could do it. And at first I simply couldn't. Georges Joubert's promise in *Savoir Skier*, the book that quickly became my ski teacher's catechism, the promise that once you start a turn, your skis will keep turning on their own, didn't seem to hold true when the new snow was knee-high. I'll never forget one particularly disastrous run from the top of the *la Berneuse* back down to the village in fresh deep powder snow. I literally crashed on every turn. Every single turn. It took more than an hour to get down to town. I would push off, pick up speed, try to turn, and crash. At least the powder was soft. I was working so hard I was soaked with sweat. Talk about paying your dues. And not surprisingly, the answer to my frustrations with powder snow, was less about technique, and more about patience, practice and keeping my balance in a new snowy environment. Letting turns happen instead of forcing them to happen. A more advanced version of the lesson I had learned on that first moonlight night beneath the American School in Leysin.

By Easter vacation, that first winter in Switzerland, I had become a skier. But I was hardly a true ski teacher, not yet anyway, even though I had actually taught a slew of spirited teenagers how to ski, giving lessons with clockwork regularity every afternoon, after the day's academic classes were done. Even so, from my very first lesson I was dead sincere about teaching, teaching well, teaching better. I think that sincerity, that caring about my students, was probably all that made my earliest lessons successful, there at the American school in Leysin, on the beginner slopes of this smallish Swiss ski resort. It seemed a miracle. My students were actually learning how to ski.

Now, looking back on that first romantic winter on skis, I can remember that my grasp of how to teach skiing was pretty sketchy. But I was hooked. Not just on skiing. Not just by those first successful days in powder snow. But by the idea of becoming a ski teacher. So much better than a real job, I told myself—meaning by that: better than an office, better than a time-clock, better than almost any other way I could think of to earn a living. And for me a special bonus of trying to earn my living as a ski teacher would be the long summers off. Time to travel and above all to climb, in mountains all around the world. The die was cast. I was almost a ski teacher. And I finished that first winter determined to become a real ski teacher.

Learning to Teach

The next year I was back in California, working in a real ski school, wearing a real ski instructor's uniform parka, teaching all day long, not just a couple of hours every afternoon, and enjoying an amazing mountain, Squaw Valley. A big mountain, very big by US standards (most resorts in the Alps are even bigger), and just what I needed: lots of experienced instructors to learn from, lots of inexperienced students to try out my new ski-teaching ideas on (real people in all sizes, shapes and ages, not just a handful of teenagers at a Swiss boarding school); and lots of amazingly steep and challenging slopes on which to hone my emerging skiing skills. The ski teaching life was as good as I had hoped it would be, maybe better. But to be honest, during those first few seasons teaching skiing at Squaw Valley, in the Lake Tahoe Sierra, I was anything but an accomplished ski instructor. I didn't know enough, I didn't have enough teaching tricks to use, I was feeling my way, class by class, student by student, day by day, into the world of effective ski teaching. And loving it. But the amazing thing is that despite my lack of experience, and lack of a deep understanding of how skiing worked, my students still learned. They learned a lot. In their eyes I wasn't a beginner at ski teaching, I was a super successful pro. How come?

Today I realize that several different things were happening that helped me succeed as a ski teacher despite my lack of skiing and teaching experience. First of course was my sincerity. I wasn't just a ski bum trying to support myself in the mountains by showing up at the ski school line-up every morning. From the beginning I really focused on my students, I wanted them to learn, to ski better. I put my heart into it, even when I was demonstrating exercises and maneuvers that I later realized weren't very helpful at all. My enthusiasm somehow carried my students forward, as we skied together on Squaw Valley's wildly diverse slopes. The fact that I believed in their ability to learn

The next year I was back in California, working in a real ski school...
...and enjoying an amazing mountain, Squaw Valley.

even more than in my own ability to teach, kept them motivated to keep trying, to keep following me, to improve their skiing performance, sometimes (I blush to admit) as a result of pure mileage on skis… That is to say, the more you ski, the less you'll fall, the easier it will feel—a kind of learning by osmosis. I was a helluva good cheerleader for my students.

But just as important as my enthusiasm, and my commitment to my students' progress was the fact that I was still learning to ski myself. Sure, after my first year in the Alps I could really fake it. My students never guessed that I was still a real newcomer to skiing. But my newly acquired skiing skills were so fresh, so tenuous, that I had no deep confidence in my own innate ability to ski well. Every time I demonstrated a turn in front of my students at Squaw Valley, a little voice inside me would whisper: "I hope this works." I was living, and teaching, and skiing with a delicious sense of constant uncertainty. My method for dealing with this strange state, strange at least for someone pretending to be a skilled professional skier, was to really pay attention to every move I made on the snow, to every sensation, to every awkward moment, to every beautiful turn. Paying attention not in a general sort of way, but in a detailed way. I was questioning, and critiquing, and monitoring my own skiing performance as much or more than that of my students.

And every breakthrough, however small, got translated into a tip, a demo, a chunk of evolving ski wisdom that I could pass on to my students. If it helped me ski better, it would surely help my students. Whatever "it" was. Paying attention to all the subtleties of one's own stance and movements is an art. It builds on your natural kinesthetic awareness, but ultimately depends on patient concentration and honest questions. In those first seasons on skis I really took the time to ask myself: Lito, are you really unweighting to make your skis turn? the way the ski school says you should? Are you really edging with your knees, the way some ski gurus said you should? Or your hips? Or your feet? Or what?...

Early on I developed the habit of taking a couple of runs all by myself, finding some empty practice terrain, blocking out all distractions and focusing on the subtle changes in weighting and stance, in movement and timing that made my turns work, or sometimes not work. And even today, decades later, I'm still my own best test subject for my evolving ski-teaching ideas. If I can't feel it, then I know I can't teach it. If I can't repeat the move, time and again, easily, then why bother presenting it to my students?

There was an interesting psychological side to my growth as a ski teacher. I am convinced that I became a very effective ski instructor because I actually experienced and felt, just what my students were experiencing and feeling – their insecurity as slopes got steeper, that moment of hesitation and anxiety before they dared to tackle a new or harder slope. I was experiencing the very same feelings. Most of my friends and fellow instructors in the Squaw Valley ski school had been skiers all their lives. Skiing for them was the most natural thing in the world. Deep down they didn't really understand why so many of their students found skiing difficult. But I did. It was a brand new experience. This gut-level empathy for insecure and tentative ski learners, in a new and sometimes daunting environment, is something that I think I held onto through all my years of teaching. Long after my own new-skier's anxieties had subsided.

Because, naturally, that state of feeling almost like an imposter, at the very least an inexperienced and uncertain skier, didn't last long. Amazing what spending every day on skis, on a great mountain, will do for one's confidence as well as one's technique.

An early lesson in confidence, and in *soft skiing* was my baptism in High Sierra deep powder skiing. Perhaps because I had fallen in love with high mountains, and mountaineering before ever starting to ski, I have always had a special thing about untracked virgin mountainsides, untracked powder snow. And Squaw Valley was the de-facto capital of Lake Tahoe powder skiing. Lots of deep snow, really deep snow, but it was heavy deep snow. As the nickname "Sierra cement" implies, new snow in the High Sierra mountains of California bears no relation to the light fluffy powder snow of the Rockies. But many of Squaw Valley's slopes are actually steep enough to let a skier move through this deep heavy snow as if it were light fluff. Skiing deep snow at Squaw is an adventure every run. That first season at Squaw, I paid a lot of dues, skied through every lunch-hour break, and by dint of trying and repetition I became a powder skier.

Toward spring I found myself in a near white-out on the flanks of KT22, the steepest peak on the long line of summits and ridges that ring Squaw Valley. It was snowing so hard I couldn't see anything. I couldn't even see how steep the West Face of KT22 really was, I had to trust myself and ski it half blind. Amazingly I did. At the bottom of KT I stopped to change my fogged-up goggles for a dry clean pair stashed inside my parka. Then it hit me. I really belonged up there. I was a skier, I wasn't faking it any longer... From that run on I had a different sense of myself, I had become a real skier, my confidence soared. Another breakthrough. Looking back it seems that this magic moment had to happen in deep and actually heavy powder. So heavy that skiers literally can't muscle their way through it. The secret of such deep snow is to just let it happen, slowly, patiently (even though you are on a steep slope). You pick up speed, give your skis a hint, a suggestion, a nudge into the beginning of a turn, and then you have to let them float around on their own. They don't betray you. Another example of *soft skiing*. And an important one because in this deep Sierra Cement you couldn't get anywhere by working too hard. You simply had to let go, and let the skis take over. One jerky, sudden or panicky movement and you would crash into this soft deep trap of Sierra cement and spend the next fifteen minutes flailing around getting back upright on your skis. *Soft skiing* was the answer.

But it took me years more before I really got my head around all the many secrets of *soft skiing*. Before I made it my core technique, my preferred style of sliding down any mountain. I won't bore you with a blow-by-blow, season-by-season account of how my skiing and my ski teaching kept changing and improving. But I would like to share one or two more special moments. Moments of particular insight. Moments when my growing understanding of skiing as a nearly effortless sport took big jumps forward.

Learning from Racers,
When They Aren't Racing.

The scene shifts. In South Lake Tahoe, high above the casinos and the neon strip at State-line where one crosses from Californian into Nevada, the slopes of Heavenly Valley hosted World Cup ski races nearly every year. For us Squaw Valley ski pros these World Cup races became a kind of annual pilgrimage. With my instructor friends I would take off, drive around the lake, and hang out alongside the steep and always icy World Cup giant-slalom course, not just as a fan, to enjoy watching the best skiers in the world, but as a serious-minded young instructor trying to learn something. If these guys are so good I reasoned (at that period Heavenly only hosted men's races) then I ought to be able to figure out exactly what they are doing, if I look hard enough, watch them carefully enough. Wrong. At least partially wrong. In those years, the late 60s and 70s, official ski technique was amazingly complicated. It was widely held that a skier had to do quite a lot to make his or her skis turn. This was the conventional wisdom, at our ski school, dispensed in how-to articles in all the ski magazines, in the official publications of ski-instructor organizations around world, American, French, Austrian, Swiss. Anyone who has skied for a long time will remember the "down—hup—and—around" mantra that instructors used to chant at their students. There was a lot of twisting, and pulling and pushing, a lot of rotation or counter-rotation, a lot of new buzzwords every season, and always the season's latest trendiest moves to learn. But it all came down to the misapprehension that one had to do something, actually do quite a lot, to make those stubborn skis turn. In all fairness, our skis in those days were a bit stubborn, relatively long and stiff. And in certain circumstances it seemed one really did have to apply a certain amount of "body English" to get those skis to cooperate. But not in powder snow. And definitiely not if you were a World Cup ski racer.

That was my big revelation at those annual races at Heavenly Valley. There they were, all my heroes, all the big names of the ski-celebrity galaxy, starting with Ingmar Stenmark, one of the two or three greatest skiers of all time. But watching individual racers flash down the icy Giant Slalom course was a frustrating experience. A couple of seconds—and pouf—the racer would disappear from sight almost before I could focus my eyes on him. So instead of just watching the race, I began to just follow these great skiers around the mountain, especially during the few hours between the first and second runs of the giant slalom competition. I watched them warm up, watched them free ski, watched them move around the mountain as if they owned it, and in a way they did. What I saw was heresy: these great skiers were not doing anything to make their skis turn. No unweighting, ("unweighting" or trying to take some weight off one's skis at the start of each turn had been the mantra of several generations of ski instructors) no up, no down, no effort. Those racers just stood there, relaxed, loose and tall, and rode their skis with the nonchalance of a ranch hand on a well-trained cutting horse. Their skis were clearly obeying them, but responding to what signals? Watching World Cup racers when they weren't racing was a powerful lesson in *soft skiing*. They were guiding their skis, I assumed, with subtle almost invisible muscular signals. Perhaps some subtle pressures inside their boots, who knows? They never lost their balance. They never seemed to do anything. Yet their skis were arcing beautiful paths down the mountain. I promised myself I would figure out how this worked. And meanwhile I recorded fantastic mental videos of *soft skiing* in action. I wasn't interested in trying to ski like these heroes through the gates and flags of an icy race course; I wanted to ski the way they did when they peeled off in lazy arcs down to the lodge for lunch. That seemed like an eminently achievable goal. Something I could do by calming down my movements, standing taller, giving my skis more time to do whatever it was that they were going to do, whatever it was that I wanted them to do, whatever it was that they wanted to do...

Without clearly understanding what I was trying to do, I simply tried to ski and look and feel like these World-Cup racers in their non-racing moments. I was playing a game with myself: let's see how little I can do, and still start a turn, still guide my turn. Sometimes it worked, sometimes not. But inevitably, as a result, I became a simpler, less flashy skier, less movement, but more results underfoot.

Lessons of a tweaked knee.

"You mean you spend all winter long skiing?" people would often ask me when they learned I was a ski instructor. "But, aren't you afraid of getting hurt?" Apparently, the image of a skier with his or her leg in a large, well-autographed plaster cast, sipping hot mulled wine in front of a lodge fireplace is a deeply ingrained part of American-skiing folklore. The answer, of course: No, I've never been afraid of getting hurt, and: Yes, it happens. Skiers do sometimes get injured, sometimes need to be taken off the mountain on a toboggan by the ski patrol. I must say that, over the years, our sport has gotten safer and safer, primarily through advances in equipment design. Especially bindings that spit you out and release your skis before those big levers can do any damage in a wild egg-beater fall. The statistics bear me out, and so does the anecdotal evidence of day after day spent on the slopes without seeing a serious accident. But accidents still happen. And the weakest link in the skier's anatomy is probably the knee. So altogether, in what today seems like a pretty long life on skis, it is hardly surprising that I have had a couple of accidents, a couple of injuries, mostly minor I'm glad to say. And hardly surprising either that the one serious injury that did put me out of commission for a whole season was an injured knee. More specifically, a burst ACL (or Anterior Cruciate Ligament) in, I think, my right knee. That was 15 years ago, and the fact that today I can't even remember whether I injured my right or my left knee should tell you that I recovered totally. I did indeed. And I owe quite a debt to orthopedic surgeons and surgery, for building me a virtual new ACL, virtually as good as my old one. It was a dumb accident. Aren't they all? I was teaching a couple of novice skiers on a freshly groomed green slope above the mid Vail restaurant, skiing quietly and probably not paying enough attention, when I looked over my shoulder at my two students, lost my balance and felt my skis slip out from under me. A second later I was sitting in the snow but still sliding forward, and as I quickly started to pull myself back up on my feet with my stomach muscles—another sensation, most unwelcome, Ouch! More like a flash of light going through me than a pain in the knee. I knew I had injured myself, but with a certain amount of macho denial I thought: Heck, maybe it's just a sprain. And I kept right on teaching. Later that morning I even taught a bump lesson. And my reasonably developed skier's leg muscles kept my knee stable, and everything worked fine...for a few more hours. But as my climbing buddy Cado always used to say, "If you don't deal with reality, reality will deal with you." And it did. By afternoon, my knee was swollen, puffed up and hurting like hell. By the next afternoon, I was in a bed in the Vail medical center recovering from successful ACL repair surgery, realizing that this particular ski season was over, and wondering how I was going to pass the months of physical therapy that I knew would be necessary to get back the full strength and mobility of my injured leg.

My grandmother used to tell me, "There's no ill but what it comes for a good reason." Did your family throw homilies like that at you? I'm not sure I ever really believed it, but sometimes it happens. In this case, those idle winter months of non-skiing pushed me to start writing my book *Breakthrough On Skis, How to Get Out of the Intermediate Rut*. That was the first silver lining, but there was another. The following season, a little nervous at first about trusting my rebuilt knee, I had a sort of on-slope epiphany. Conversations with my knee surgeon had convinced me that the most physically stressful aspect of modern skiing, and the kind of skiing most likely to re-injure my newly rebuilt knee was bump or mogul skiing. Problem was, I loved bump skiing. The quickness. The challenge. The excitement of diving into a mogul field and skiing it well. I had never paid much attention to the occasional thump, or bump, the occasional shock of hitting a mogul wrong, of finding myself sometimes—after losing the line—skiing at cross-purposes to the bumpy terrain. But now I realized that with a theoretically weaker knee after my accident and surgery, I would have to totally change my way of bump skiing. I would have to become a lot better, and a lot smoother. If I wanted to keep on skiing bumps, I needed to become a silky smooth bump skier and learn how to avoid all the thumping and hammering usually associated with moguls.

A big order, but by the end of the following season I was a different skier. It was *soft skiing* squared. I was able to take the general idea of letting skis and mountain interact to do the job, and distill it into a bump skiing pattern where the shape of the bump does the whole job, or at least more than 90% of it. Bump skiing became something relaxing, I stopped thumping into bumps, and my knees thanked me for it. So my tweaked and repaired knee not only forced me to become a better skier, it made me a better ski teacher because it was obvious that my students, very average folks, not young athletic heroes, weren't looking to pound their way down steep bump slopes at high speeds. They wanted what I wanted—a way to ski bumpy slopes with grace and ease, at comfortable speeds, even slow speeds. Why not? The actual tricks I developed for making friends with bumps are a little too complex to summarize in a short paragraph. I devoted a big chapter to smooth bump skiing in my last book, *Breakthrough on the New Skis*, and mastering bumps is not really the goal of this book. Suffice it to say, that the soft approach to bump skiing involves relaxing and loosening up one's feet, letting one's skis slip and slide through the sinuous troughs of a mogul field, not pushing and jamming one's skis from turn to turn, bump to bump. Flowing down a bump run is a tricky but logical extension of *soft skiing.*

Occam's Razor,
a Philosophy of Minimalist Skiing

From the World Cup racers at Heavenly Valley, to the gentler style of bump skiing I started to work on after busting my ACL, there was a constant thread, a steady goal, and eventually a single result: *Do less!* Get the most out of my skis with the least effort, the very least effort. Sometimes I have felt almost guilty pursuing this goal. Isn't skiing a sport? Isn't it in the nature and essence of sport that one should make a serious, sustained, or sometimes even explosive physical effort? Usually that's the case. But there are sports and then there are sports. Aerobic sports are indeed sports that reward the participant for doing more, or for training to be able to do more. Running, swimming, rock climbing. You know what I am talking about. Self-powered sports. But skiing (downhill skiing not cross-country skiing) is different. It isn't a self-powered sport at all. A skier's movement down the mountain is a gift, a gift of gravity, pulling us down an inclined plane. It's simple, and it's free.

The skier's role, I came to understand more and more clearly, winter by winter, is to balance and adjust those outside forces: the pull of gravity, the resistance of the snow against our skis. And ultimately not merely to balance and adjust and control these forces, but to play with them. Skiing then, as I have learned it and practiced it and taught it for years, is more like a game than a normal sport. A creative and liberating game. A game without rules or referees. A game you can play with the mountain, with winter, every time you step onto a pair of skis. A game that awards no extra points for doing more.

That's why I have pursued a kind of minimalist approach to skiing and teaching skiing. Do less, teach less. Only what is absolutely necessary to make this turn, that run. Only what is necessary to handle today's snow conditions, not all snow conditions. Some slopes, some snow, some days make skiing harder, and yes, maybe we need to do a little more. Maybe. But the essence of *soft skiing*, the theme of this book, is to relax and enjoy the ride down the mountain. And use as little technique as possible to make it happen. Occam's Razor is a pragmatic but philosophical principle attributed to a 14th century logician, William of Ockham, that suggests that among several explanations, or choices, it always makes sense to select the simplest one. Seems to me that this "razor" for slicing through confusion, can be applied to skiing, to ski technique, and to ski teaching. Why do skis turn? How do skiers turn? Always go with the simplest explanation. How can I teach someone to ski like I do, like an expert? Go with the simplest possible instructions. Whenever possible, do less. That's what *soft skiing* is all about.

Pogo's Lesson:
"We have met the enemy....

Do you remember Walt Kelly's adorable fuzzy cartoon character, the wise little possum Pogo? The Pogo comic strip stopped publication in 1975 but the character Pogo remains an American original. Pogo's arguably most memorable dictum, "We have met the enemy and he is us," explains why we can't always ski our best, despite all our technique, all our mastery of the secrets of *soft skiing*. And Pogo's observation holds true for everyone, for all skiers. Certainly for me, and I'll bet for you too.

What happens is this: inevitably, when you venture outside your comfort zone on the mountain, you tense up. Everyone does. Excess muscular tension, which is almost always the result of extra mental tension, is the worst enemy of *soft skiing*. Your movements become excessive and jerky, your skis over-edge and catch, your balance is compromised. Everything goes to hell, and you find yourself simply unable to ski your best. I can't tell you how may times this has happened to me, on particularly steep and daunting slopes.

In the ski teaching world, the notion of a skier's "comfort zone" is commonplace. An expert skier has a comfort zone, just as a hesitant novice skier does. And beyond the limits of this comfort zone, lies trouble. Trouble for the expert as well as the novice or intermediate. My own limits of comfortable skiing are pretty high. I can handle and enjoy quite difficult slopes and ski them in a relaxed manner with a smile plastered all over my face. But at a certain point—*whoa!*—I tense up and my technique goes all to hell. Good skiing, brilliant skiing, *soft skiing*, happens when a skier can relax and let go. Relax and let go—these few words are both a psychological and also a physical and physiological recipe.

In Part II we will focus on the importance of muscular relaxation, selective relaxation, and the release of muscle tension as a key technique in *soft skiing*—as the best way to launch a smooth, graceful, efficient ski turn. But for now, let me just emphasize this final lesson in my own skiing apprenticeship. The limits of even an expert skier's technique are the limits of relaxation. When you tense up, it's "Game Over."

I got the best possible demonstration of this idea a few years ago, skiing with a fellow Aspen ski pro, Charlie MacArthur on a very, very steep bump slope at Snowmass. Not a dangerous slope but definitely steep enough to really get your attention—steep enough that I couldn't help feeling just a little proud of my own ability to ski it well, under control, with continuous linked turns. But right beside me, there was Charlie, and I couldn't take my eyes off him. He wasn't taking this slope seriously, he was laughing, playing with those monstrous bumps. He looked like a rubber man, every part of his body was so loose, so relaxed. I could tell that his skis never ever caught, never jammed into a bump, never over-edged coming out of a turn. There was no separating one turn from the next. Charlie's skis simply slipped from bump to bump, flowing through and around those bumps like water. Charlie, of course, was and is a phenomenal athlete, equally gifted on telemark skis, or in a whitewater kayak amid tons of crashing water, and also a member of the US demo ski team. He was so far *inside* his comfort zone that he hadn't even noticed that this slope was difficult. The difference between his turns and mine was 100% due to the difference between his total relaxation and my more cautious muscle tension on this rather challenging run. I could see it. And although I couldn't change it then and there, it gave me another dimension of *soft skiing* to work on and develop. And ultimately to try to pass on to my students.

Once the basic moves are there, once you've mastered and integrated the soft approach to expert skiing, all that stands between you and a perfect run, on the hardest of slopes, is you. I know that it's no use just telling myself to relax on scary steep slopes, right at my limit. No use beating myself up. Instead I've learned that I have to patiently train myself, or trick myself, into becoming an ever more confident, hence ever more relaxed skier. It's a goal I have long pursued, am still pursuing, and I am happy to report that it works. The limits of my comfort zone today are a lot higher than they used to be. And the best news is that what I've described as *soft skiing* works amazingly well in even the most challenging situations. *Soft skiing down hard slopes!*

How did I do it? Much more importantly: How are you going to do it? We'll explore this final step together, after we have looked at—and mastered—the basics of *soft skiing* in the next section of this book—*Your Story*.

You don't have to be a superb athlete to become an expert skier....

Part II
YOUR STORY
HOW YOU CAN MASTER
THE SKILLS OF SOFT SKIING

The proof that expert skiing is a lot easier than anyone imagines—I always used to tell my students—is that I myself and so many of my ski-instructor buddies have become expert skiers without ever possessing any special athletic ability. If it was really hard, like being a brilliant basketball player, or gymnast, I'm sure I couldn't do it. Most of my friends couldn't either. You don't have to be a superb athlete to become an expert skier, although clearly the ski racers we sometimes watch on television (at least every four years at the Olympics) are indeed superb athletes.

What I call *soft skiing*—skiing in such a way that you, the skier, are using little or no muscular force to make things happen but are instead relying on ski design, on the shape of the mountain, plus patience and subtlety to create beautiful runs—is actually nothing more than relaxed expert skiing, period. I am an expert skier and I'm also a bit lazy. We all are. Why work at skiing? Why work any harder than you absolutely have to, to slide down the mountain? So sometimes in this next section I will simply talk about "expert skiing," and sometimes I will focus on why I call my particular style of expert skiing *soft skiing*, but it's all the same beautiful effortless dance with the mountain.

My sense is that *soft skiing* (that is to say, skiing like a very relaxed expert) depends on a few simple and easy-to-master moves. Let's start with the most basic, and fortunately the simplest of these: *standing* and *walking*. Not just plain old standing and everyday walking, but standing like an expert skier, and then "walking" into your turns. And let's begin with the way you stand on your skis.

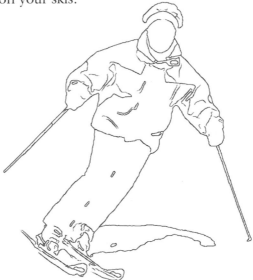

Standing

Expert skiers stand taller. They never hunker down to lower their center of gravity, and they don't spread their legs, feet and skis apart in order to feel more stable and secure. But how then do they keep their balance? How exactly do they feel so solid and secure on their skis? Easy. *Expert skiers balance with their hands.*

In fact, if you were trying to put the whole story of modern skiing into one small sentence—an enormous oversimplification, I know—you could put it this way: *experts balance with their hands and they ski with their feet.*

But let's stick with balance for a moment. I want to make sure you have a good mental image of what "balancing with your hands" really means. Imagine a young boy trying to walk along the top of a small fence, or say walk along a 2x4 on the ground, or maybe even balancing along on a railroad track. Would this kid keep his hands at his side? or in his pockets? No way. He would spread his hands out to each side and make very small balancing movements with them to compensate for any shift in balance as he walked along that rail. You can try this yourself by walking carefully along a straight crack in a sidewalk. You will probably spread your hands naturally to either side to balance. Even if it doesn't seem natural in your case, make sure that you do it. This is a vitally important habit to get into on the slopes.

In short, balancing almost always requires that we spread something. Beginners spread their feet and skis, creating a wide pyramidal shape that simply can't get knocked over. But from such a wide stance it is very difficult to move gracefully in any direction. Experts on the other hand, stand tall and loose, and spread their hands, not their skis, for balance. Why does this work so well? Simple. Your hands are very light, and very mobile; you can easily move them in any direction, wherever you want. But your hands are also at the ends of two very long levers, your arms. And this makes any small adjustment of your hand position very effective.

Let's go one step further before we leave this critical notion of balancing with our hands. A skier's balance is challenged in more than one dimension, more than one direction. Spreading your hands laterally will improve your lateral, or side-to-side balance. But how about fore-and-aft balance? Something else is going on all the time on the slopes. Every time we point our skis a bit more down the hill, they speed up. The effect is as though they were trying to run out from underneath us. This is why so many skiers wind up sitting back, with their weight on their heels, or worse. "In the back seat" as instructors sometimes say. The answer is simple in theory: as our skis speed up underneath us we should just lean forward a bit, to keep up with them, to stay centered, to stay in good fore-and-aft balance. Easier said than done. Luckily there is a trick. To lean forward, or to put it in techie-sounding language, to move your center of gravity forward to keep up with your skis, just reach your hands a bit further forward.

It's uncanny. You will find that your hands are like magnets. Move them and your body follows, easily, effortlessly, not even consciously. So the whole story about balancing with your hands is really this. Carry your hands spread out to the side and always ahead of your hips. That's it. With your hands around waist-level in height, spread them and reach forward. That is precisely how expert skiers maintain their balance. That's how I want you to find and keep something like perfect balance over your skis. As you will soon discover, it works beautifully. There is only one rub to this all important balancing trick. It doesn't feel natural.

At least not at first. In our everyday life, far from the slopes, we mostly keep our hands at our sides. We don't walk around with our hands and arms spread out to the side and reaching forward. So it will take a bit of doing, a bit of repetition, to make this a habit. But it is one of the best habits a skier can build.

Imagine you are at a party, helping the hostess serve a tray of drinks. You grab the tray and walk around chatting with the other guests. Your hands holding the tray are both spread wide and held in front of you. That's exactly how you will balance on your skis, not just on easy green slopes, or just on hard black slopes, but on all slopes, all the time. And yet, if you put that tray of drinks down and walked around the room with your arms held out in that position, your friends would surely raise an eyebrow. Oh you poor dear, what happened? See what I mean? It isn't natural. But that is one of your first tasks in pursuit of efficient graceful well balanced skiing. Make this "balancing hand position" into a habit by concentrating on it for a few runs, a few days, however long it takes...

Walking

So much for an efficient skier's stance: tall not hunkered down, with hands spread and reaching forward. Now, with that stance as a kind of home base, how are you going to move, and move your skis, to create those swooping graceful effortless runs that we all have in mind? To answer this question let's take a small detour. Of all the possible actions the human body is capable of, what do we do more than anything else? What have we done all our lives?

Every day, rain or shine. Why, walking of course. No, I'm not kidding, we are about to explore the crucial and subtle relation between walking and modern skiing. But let's tie walking into our discussion of balance. When I think about walking in relation to what we do on skis, I am thinking in particular of what might be called foot-to-foot balancing. Moving easily and naturally, as we walk, from one foot to another and finding ourselves in perfect balance over the new foot, as we move onto it. Isn't that what we do when we walk down the street? Or walk across the room? Of course it is. We are going to take that obvious, almost trivial motor skill of walking, a skill that we all possess and subtly blend it into a movement pattern that will eventually give us total and, yes, effortless, control over our skis.

Start the process of "ski walking" like this. Stand up, wherever you are, and instead of walking forward, just imagine that you are walking forward but actually walk slowly in place. Simply step lightly and easily from foot to foot, as though you were walking forward. Easy, wasn't it? Now the same thing only slower, and then again, slower still. As though you were walking in glue, or maybe, for a more pleasing image as though you were stepping from foot to foot, chest deep in water in the shallow end of a swimming pool—with the resistance of the water slowing down your movements. Skiing on packed slopes, as we are about to see, has a lot to do with this kind of slow-motion stepping from foot to foot. Why? How? I can almost hear the chorus of questions. But before I pull back the curtain and show why this kind of movement is so important in *soft skiing*, let's go a little further.

I began by asking you to "walk" in place, in your home, in your office, wherever you happen to be. Next I asked you to slow this foot-to-foot, side-to-side movement down, slowing the pace until you are moving from foot to foot a good deal more slowly than when you actually walk forward. Finally, now, I am going to ask you to do the same thing, only without lifting your feet off the ground. A funny kind of walking you are thinking, but heck, it started out as walking in place. It is the same sort of movement, only less, and of course slower. So now you are—what should we call it? simply shifting your weight smoothly, easily and slowly from foot to foot, from side to side. That's it.

And now, before I lose you to boredom, let me fill in one more part of the puzzle, which will make it clear why this sort of slow-motion, in-place "walking", or as we often say in skier's shorthand, "weight-shift" is so important. The missing piece of the puzzle is an explanation of why our skis turn.

Turning
And Why our Skis Turn

Already, in Part I, I talked a lot about letting our skis do all the work for us. About starting a turn and letting it continue *on its own*. I have hinted, even asserted, that our skis are designed this way, designed to turn for us. I want you not only to believe me, but to have a clear mental picture of just how and why this is so. How it works. So let's look a little closer.

In the final analysis, a ski is much more than a fancy board with a turned-up tip. The sides of our skis have a very graceful, and very clever, curved shape. A much more pronounced side curve today than 10, 15, 20 years ago; but even so, skis have had a definite curve to their sides for over a hundred years. And this is what makes them turn for us. Skis are widest up front, they narrow considerably underfoot, then flare out wide again toward the rear or tail end, but not as wide as at the front. The combination of the wider front end, and the more-or-less deep curving-in at the middle or waist of the ski makes our skis tend to follow an arc on the snow. There are actually two different principles at work here. The wide tip of the ski allows us to skid or slip in an arc. The narrow waist of the ski is what allows the ski to "carve" a turn. But perhaps not surprisingly, most turns are the to result of both factors, both principles. When one factor dominates, we get a very skidded turn; when the other dominates, the result is a very carved turn. And as I just hinted, most turns have a bit of skidding, and bit of carving in them, in varying proportions. Let's look at each factor separately. But I promise you, no physics, no equations. So bear with me.

The Skidded Turn principle. Skidded or slipped turns depend almost exclusively on the fact that the front of the ski is wider than the middle or the tail of the ski. If you place or twist your ski, even slightly, across the direction you are moving, and put it on edge, that ski is going to skid. However, being wider, the tip digs into the snow a bit harder and deeper than the rest of the ski and creates extra friction. That extra friction slows the tip of the ski relative to the tail which slides out to the side a

In a skidded or "slipped" turn, the tail of the ski slides out to the side while the ski continues to move forward, producing an arc.

bit more. But while the tail of the ski is slipping out to the side, the ski is still moving forward, and this combination of the tail slipping sideways while the ski moves forward produces an arc. See the drawing above. This is perhaps easier to grasp in a drawing than to explain in words but you should think of these two movements happening at the same time, the tail slipping out to the side while the ski keeps moving ahead. The result is a nice round skidded turn. This is the kind of turn a lot of skiers, maybe most skiers, make. For much of the 20th century this was *the way* skis turned. Period.

The Carved Turn principle. But there is something else going on, especially with modern skis, in modern carved turns. When the deeply curved side of a ski is tilted up onto its edge, then it seems logical that that narrow center section would be lifted clean off the snow. Would be that is, if you weren't standing on it. But the weight of a skier presses the center of the ski back into the snow, actually bends the ski into a slightly bowed shape, an actual curve in the snow. See the drawing below. And if you let your ski follow this curve with no additional twisting, you will experience a so-called carved turn. "Carving a turn" has to be one of the most elegant moves, and one of the best feelings in modern skiing. In fact ski racers have carved their turns for generations, but it was only with the development of shorter skis with a deeper side curve or side cut, that carving became a real option for the rest of us.

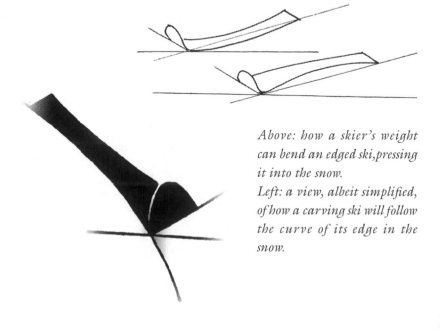

Above: how a skier's weight can bend an edged ski, pressing it into the snow.
Left: a view, albeit simplified, of how a carving ski will follow the curve of its edge in the snow.

One can summarize this necessarily complex explanation of the modern turn, as I did in my first Breakthrough On Skis video by saying: "Skis turn best when they are bent, and the best way to bend a ski is to put all your weight on it."

But it bears repeating, once again, whether our skis are skidding through an arc, or carving around that arc, or most likely a subtle combination of the two, it is the ski that is turning, not the skier. The ski turns, you don't.

OK. That's the story, a more-or-less simple explanation of why our skis turn for us. But we need one more piece of the puzzle. Just what is the skier's role? What do we need to do to make our skis do their thing? How do we make them turn for us, in the most efficient way, with the least effort? How do we trigger, and then subtly adjust and control our skis' own built-in tendency to turn?

Putting It All Together
Walking in Slow-motion into a Turn

You are moving over the snow, and you want to turn. Say you want to turn to the left. Smoothly and easily (remember that gentle slow-motion walking exercise a few paragraphs earlier) shift all your weight onto your right foot. Walk onto your right foot, and just stay there, balanced, waiting, for an extra a second or two.

What happens? As you shift *onto* your right foot, you are also—automatically—shifting *off* your left foot. With less support on the left side, your whole body will tilt, ever so slightly, to the left—this just happens, by itself, automatically—which in turn tilts your right ski slightly onto its edge. And then, with all your weight now on one ski, that right ski bends and bites into the snow more than before. Voila, a turn begins. Sure, it's a slow turn. We like it that way. You feel the ski start to arc around to the left, and with a smile on your lips you ride that ski through a long slow beautiful arc. A perfect long radius turn. At least that's the way it should feel, and will feel as you tune in to this style of turning. Not by twisting your skis into a new direction, but by shifting (walking) onto one ski, which bends, dominates, and carries you in an unhurried arc.

Unhurried is the key. I hope you will practice this, and play around with this idea of shifting weight from foot to foot in a kind of patient slow-motion walking action, on a wide, groomed and very easy slope. This is a strategy we will use to practice almost every new move I suggest. That is to say, I want you to pick a practice slope with lots of space and no inherent challenge. A place where you don't really have to turn. Where you can afford to wait, patiently, and see if, after a pregnant pause, your skis (and in particular the ski you are now standing on) really will start to turn. And then keep on turning.

I am assuming that most, if not all, of those who will read this book are actually skiers of one stripe or another. At least you have skied a bit, even if you never made that heady breakthrough into the world of effortless expert skiing. That means, of course, that you will already have developed quite a few skiing "habits," and probably not very good habits. When most average ho-hum intermediate skiers want to make a turn, what do they do? Typically, they twist their skis, more or less vigorously in the direction they want to go. And it works. They skid sideways a bit, then the skis grab and off they go in the new direction. I am suggesting something quite different. Making a turn without twisting your skis at all. Stepping onto one ski and waiting....

Once you have felt this new sensation, your skis carrying you slowly around a big turn with precious little or no effort on your part, go with it. Keep playing around with the sensation of walking in slow motion from ski to ski. Not striding from ski to ski but shifting smoothly, from ski to ski. Do it to both sides. Do it again and again...and yet again. Don't rush off in search of steeper slopes. Stay on a relaxing open groomed green slope a little longer than you usually would. Savoring the sensation of slowly arcing skis.

While we are at it, let's make sure we are all talking the same language when it comes to turning. Skiers have a whole raft of shorthand code words for talking about their sport, and for describing which ski is doing what. If you are sliding across a slope, not straight down but across the hill, we say you are "traversing" the slope. In a "traverse," one ski will always be higher than the other on the snow. And in this case, we can always talk about your uphill ski or your downhill ski. But in a turn, things aren't that simple. Your uphill ski at the start of a turn will soon become your downhill ski as you finish the turn heading back across the hill in the opposite direction. So we prefer to talk about the "inside" and "outside" ski of a turn. I'll use these terms a lot, so take a moment to be sure you have clear picture of what I mean.

If you think of a turn on the snow as an arc, part of a circle, then one ski will always be on the outside of that arc, on the outside of that imaginary circle. And the other ski will be on the inside. So if you are going to make a turn to the left, your left ski will be the "inside ski," and your right ski will be the "outside ski." Simple, no? But important, because in the majority of turns, the outside ski and the inside ski have a very different role to play. When I talk about "walking in slow motion into a turn," I am talking about shifting your weight, easily and smoothly, like walking, onto the ski that will become the outside ski of your turn. That ski bites deeper into the snow, it bends, it brings you around. In other words, the outside ski is responsible for creating the turn.

Now that we share this important bit of ski vocabulary, we can go on and look more closely, more carefully, at the style of big round easy turns that we want to develop and practice.

Patience, the Key to Soft Skiing
Waiting for the Turn to Happen

Close your eyes for a moment and try to call up a mental picture of a couple of expert skiers, sailing past you on friendly terrain, relaxed, effortless, looking for all the world as though they owned the mountain. I'd be willing to bet that although these skiers are traveling rapidly down the mountain, their own movements are slow, smooth and unhurried. They never seem to jerk their skis around at the last minute. Everything about these experts seems to express confidence, in particular, confidence that their skis are going to turn, when and where they want them to.

More than once I have been tempted to say that the key skill in modern expert skiing is patience, although I know that would be a ridiculous oversimplification. Yet patience really is an incredibly important part of the way we ski. In particular at the start of every turn. Waiting for the turn to happen, not rushing it. The patience to let the ski bend, bite, and peel off into an arc, on its own. Without helping it, without a little extra twisting on our part.

I want to avoid a potential misunderstanding here. I am not talking about every possible turn on every possible slope. There are some tight situations—steep and gnarly bumps are a perfect example—where a skier will have to twist his or her skis quickly into a new turn, without hesitation, without waiting. Last minute action to save the day. But the mental picture and the skiing pattern that I want to share with you here is all about what is often called "cruising skiing." Graceful smooth runs down wide-open slopes where each turn is an extended pleasure, not a crisis. I want to convince you to make this sort of big, slow, "cruising" turn into your basic turn—a kind of home-base technique that you come back to again and again.

These turns will be medium to long-radius turns, unhurried arcs, where you, the skier, feel like a privileged passenger, riding a well-trained ski around an almost predestined arc. In this sense, when I talk about patience in connection with *soft skiing*, I mean the patience to wait for the turn to start, on its own. You shift smoothly onto a new ski, the ski that will soon be the outside ski of the coming turn, and you wait for something to happen. It always does.

But how long do you have to wait? How long should you wait after "walking" smoothly onto that new ski?

Step.........and.........then the turn starts

It's only a slight hesitation, a slight pause in the action. The best way I can describe this slight hesitation, this slight pause, is to say that it feels very much like an extra beat in music. The rhythm at the start of a big easy turn is: step—**and**—turn. Where that "*and*" is like a gentle breath, or as I just suggested, an extra beat in a piece of music. Think one...*and*...two. Step...*and*... turn. Shift...*and*...turn. And always, that "*and*" will be a brief but delicious pause in the action. A brief moment where nothing happens, although everything is about to happen. This kind of patience is also a real commitment. You simply have to *believe* in it. And that is why I asked you to practice this sort of turn on a wide-open, easy, groomed slope, the sort of terrain where you don't absolutely need to turn. Where you can afford to experiment with this kind of patience, with this brief moment of simply waiting to see whether or not your turn will start. Trust me, it will. If I asked you to try this on a steep, challenging, or scary slope, it couldn't possibly work. A kind of self-preservation instinct would make you twist those skis around, fast.

But once you have felt this sort of gentle, automatic, smooth, long-radius turn, a turn that feels as though it was happening without you, I want you to keep going. Keep making these big easy turns, one after the other, one run after another, until they begin to feel totally natural, until they become a sort of habit. No, you don't have to spend all day, every day, on easy groomed green slopes, it could quickly become boring. But do spend enough time on easy slopes, repeating this kind of easy, slow-to-start turn to do the job, to build some brand new, expert habits. To make friends with this easy, automatic, long-radius turn that happens simply because you stand more solidly on one ski than on the other.

Soft Weight Shift
The Crucial Role of Relaxation.

Weight-shift by any other name is still weight-shift. And when I asked you to practice "walking" in slow-motion onto your new ski, the new outside ski of the coming turn, that was just another way of talking about weight-shift. Just another image, and I hope a good one, for weight-shift. Shifting your weight from ski to ski to make something happen. I like the notion of "walking from ski to ski" because it ties skiing and weight-shift into some basic motor skills that we have been practicing, so to speak, all our lives. Nothing could be more basic than walking. We all know how to move efficiently from one foot to another when we are walking down the street. So I wanted to connect you with those same reflexes, that same easy foot-to-foot balance when you find yourself on your skis. Looked at in those terms, skiing doesn't seem like such a strange activity.

But there is one rub, one flaw with my image or metaphor of walking for weight-shift. Walking, real-life walking that is, involves picking your feet up off the ground. Yet in modern expert skiing we very seldom lift a foot, a boot or a ski off the snow. Why not?

The answer is deceptively simple. Good skiers, expert skiers, are also in a sense a bit lazy. Typically they don't want to work any harder than they absolutely need to in order to make their skis behave. On a packed slope, when I move smoothly from one arc to another, one turn to the next, it is true that I am always shifting my body weight to the new outside ski of the coming turn. Putting more weight onto one ski, of course, means taking that weight off the other ski, off the inside ski of this coming turn. Thus one ski is heavy, biting into the snow, doing its job, while the other ski (on the inside of the arc) is light, just floating through the turn. If we were skiing together I could easily prove to you that all my weight was on my outside ski simply by lifting my light inside ski up off the snow. But if that ski is really light—and indeed it is—lifting it up off the snow won't make it any lighter. That's why, like most expert skiers, I just leave both skis on the snow. It saves energy, to be sure. But unfortunately it can also create confusion because, usually, you can't see me shift my weight from ski to ski, foot to foot, when I start an easy long turn. In fact, this is the source of endless misunderstandings about modern skiing. *If you can't see it, is it really happening?* If you can't see skiers shift their weight from foot to foot, ski to ski, at the start of each turn, then how do you know they are really doing it? Let's look at this conundrum a little closer.

Many contemporary ski instructors will tell you that weight-shift is no longer cool, is no longer necessary, no longer an essential part of expert technique. I beg to differ. If we were scientists, looking for an experiment to see just where experts put their weight—predominantly on one ski, or equally on both skis—we could go out and look at the tracks that expert skiers leave in the snow. Even when hyper-modern hot shots are leaving "railroad tracks" in the snow (one of the apparent hallmarks of pure carved turns) it is easy to see that the outside ski is biting more deeply into the snow than the one on the inside of the turn. Or one could look at still photos taken in a high-speed sequence showing experts carving beautiful turns; or perhaps slow-motion films of those same experts arcing beautiful turns down the mountain. And we would see that the outside ski of their turn is almost always bent into more of an arc than the other ski. Bent because it bears more weight. But really we are just skiers, not scientists; we aren't here to prove anything.

After all the years I have spent on skis, today I can easily make turns with most or all of my weight on the outside ski, or with my weight equally distributed over both skis. Or even, as silly as it sounds, make turns with all my weight on my inside ski. I can, but I don't. Turning on packed slopes with virtually all your weight on the outside ski of the arc (weight-shift by any other name) is simply easier, more relaxing, and for me, more graceful and efficient. It is the way I prefer to ski. So let me suggest this: When someone tells you that weight-shift onto the outside ski is *passé*, or old-fashioned, or no longer needed with today's skis, just keep your counsel, smile, try out the moves they suggest, and then stick with whatever works best for you. I am willing to bet that you will continue shifting your weight gracefully to your new outside ski. It works so well. Why change for something much trickier?

But as I pointed out, only a paragraph ago, most of the time you won't see expert skiers actually stepping, or visibly moving onto their new outside ski. For all the world it looks as if these experts are just standing squarely on two very cooperative skis. How then are they shifting their weight from one ski to the other? That same question is still hanging in the air: *if you can't see it, is it really happening.* The answer in this case is a resounding *Yes.* And here is how it works:

When I shift from one ski to the other to start a new turn, I use a subtle trick that I call *soft weight-shift.* By soft weight-shift I mean weight-shift through relaxation, by subtly relaxing certain muscles, but not others. You see, in order to support the weight of your body, the muscles in your legs need to be somewhat tense, because in a sense they are actually holding you up against the pull of gravity. At the very least, those slightly tense leg muscles are supporting the framework of bones, your leg bones, which in turn support your weight.

So let's suppose you are sliding down and across the slope, a comfortable traverse on a comfortable slope, heading down and left. Probably much if not all of your weight will be on your lower ski, your right ski. So your right leg is really doing the work of supporting your body weight. Now.... Suppose you quickly relax the muscles in that right leg, including the muscles in your right foot. What happens? Your right leg, now relaxed, is no longer doing its job of holding you up, and so your weight smoothly and easily (and automatically) shifts to your other leg. Your body simply will never let you collapse when you relax the supporting muscles on one side; the other side always takes up the slack. What happens then? You already know the answer don't you? Without that support on the downhill side your whole body starts to tilt gently to that side, downhill, and your top ski, your left ski, now bearing your weight rolls over onto its edge, bends and bites into the snow, and that long graceful turn begins. Of course, that's a full written-out description. But in much less time than it took me to write those sentences, or you to read them, you have almost automatically started a smooth long turn. That same familiar rhythm, with that same familiar mini pause: *shift weight—and—turn*. Only this time the weight-shift happened by relaxation, by relaxing your downhill foot and leg. Cool. Someone watching you wouldn't have seen any obvious sign of weight-shift. No stepping from ski to ski, certainly no movement from one side to the other, no clue. But you felt it. As you relaxed one foot and leg, the other side took over and the turn started. Seemingly by itself. This kind of weight-shift that I call *soft weight-shift*—weight-shift by relaxing the leg muscles on the inside of your intended turn—is surely the biggest secret in modern skiing. Now you know.

But knowing and doing are two different things. How are we going to train your muscles, your feet and legs, so that this efficient virtually effortless form of weight-shift becomes a habit? As easy to trigger as just thinking: "let's turn." Or maybe not thinking at all. As usual, we are going to tackle this in stages. Starting right now, at home, before you ever reach the slopes and step into your skis.

Start with this small exercise to feel, really feel, the difference between tense muscles and totally lose relaxed ones. Hold up one hand and look at it. Then make a gentle fist; just close your fingers into the shape of a fist but don't squeeze. Next squeeze that fist very tightly so you can really feel your hand and fingers as tense as possible. Squeeze that fist so tightly that it almost trembles. Then, after a moment of this, say after counting to three, quickly open your hand and shake your fingers out, loosely, with a floppy shaking movement at the wrist. By doing this, you have just experienced the two extremes of total muscular tension and its opposite, total muscular relaxation. It is rather easy to see, to control and feel these extremes in your hand, held up in front of your face. Do this a couple of times, without questioning too much whether it really makes sense. Inevitably, as you do this, you will start to acquire a certain sort of kinesthetic awareness of tension vs. relaxation.

Next of course, we want to experience something very similar in the muscles of one foot and leg. This is not quite as obvious. But once again, I have a sort of in-place exercise to propose: Do this one standing in front of the kitchen sink, or maybe in front of a bureau or chest of drawers. Face the sink or chest of drawers and put your hands on its edge for a little extra balance. Stand with your weight on both feet equally. Then focus on your right foot, and see if you can tighten up the muscles in your feet (of course these muscles run up into your leg too). This tightening action feels almost as though you are trying to lift the toes of that foot off the ground. You will feel the muscle tension from your foot go right up into your leg. As you do this, it will probably feel as though your tightening up of one foot is actually starting to lift the other foot slightly. Now, all at once, relax that tension. Feel your foot go soft, just as your fingers did in the tight-fist exercise. And feel that your whole right leg gets suddenly loose, or "gives," or folds a bit. Of course, you will also feel your weight sort of plop down on your other foot, as that other leg, your left leg, tenses or gets stronger to support your weight. Do this a couple of times, alternating the foot that you first tighten, and then loosen. The important part of this small exercise is not the tightening-up action, but the letting go, the relaxing. I am only asking you to tighten your muscles first, in these exercises, in order to help you feel the difference when you relax them a moment later.

Relaxation is the key. Sometimes I talk about "differential relaxation" because we need to learn to relax the muscle tension in one foot and leg, but not in the other. This is not something we do very much in everyday life. It isn't hard. It's just new. And you need to build up a certain awareness, a feel for what is going on down there close to the snow. Ultimately *soft weight-shift*, getting your weight off one ski by simply relaxing that foot and leg, is going to become your basic habit, your basic "move" for triggering turns. We really need to relax the whole leg on the inside of the coming turn, so that the outside leg, foot and ski receive all our body weight. But even though the whole leg is involved in this "action," I want you to begin by focusing on your feet. Your feet are very sensitive and, so to speak, lead the process. I am sure you will be able to feel this at home, this loosening, or giving, or squishing, or soft folding of one leg via muscular relaxation. But in the end the important thing is to feel it, and do it, and enjoy the result—a free turn—out on the slopes. So back to our skis.

The skier's body starts to "fall" or tilt to the right...

The right foot and leg both relax

Now the left ski is weighted, and starts to roll on to its edge.

A smooth turn begins

Play with soft weight-shift first on an easy groomed slope. Head almost straight down the hill, pretty fast. As smoothly as you can let one foot and leg just go limp, relaxed and soft. A turn starts, right? Remember, this is an easy turn on an easy slope, not a do-or-die crisis turn on a steep and scary slope. That will come later, much later. The feeling, however, of relaxing one foot and leg, and feeling your skis turn in that direction is really an eye opener, really sublime. Once you have felt it, I want you to play with this sensation for at least several runs. On a wide green slope or an easy blue one.

As with our initial walking-into-weight-shift turns, there is a pause. A delicious split second of uncertainty and hesitation. Will my skis turn or not? They always do. And the rhythm is always the same. Whether we think of it as shift-*and*-turn, or relax-*and*-turn, that mini pause, that "*and*" is important. Remember how much stress I put on patience. Perhaps starting a turn with *soft weight-shift* requires even more patience. Because if you think about weight-shift in terms of simply walking, or stepping onto the new ski, then at least that stepping seems to be a definite, positive action, something that you, the skier, actually do. But is relaxing one foot and leg really an action? Or more a kind of non-action, or anti-action? However you think of it, *soft weight-shift*, weight-shift by relaxing one leg, represents a breakthrough, a revolutionary approach to making your skis turn, almost a case of getting something for nothing.

Remember that I confessed earlier that I was a rather lazy expert skier. Why work harder than I have to? I think a lot of gifted expert skiers share this same sort of laziness. Or, to make it sound a bit spiffier, let's call it a search for efficiency. An answer to the question: how can I get the most from my skis with the least amount of input and effort on my part. A sort of minimalist approach to starting turns. If that sounds attractive reading this page, let me tell you it is even better out on the hill, flying along, the wind in your face, a perfect winter day. You feel like turning left, you simply relax your left foot and leg, you let that leg "give," or gently flex, or fold, ever so slightly, and the other leg, foot and ski take over and guide you around in a beautiful arc. You enjoy the curve, the arcing ride, and then you're ready to do it again, on the other side...

You feel like turning left, you simply relax your left foot and leg...

You'll have noticed perhaps that I am often using different words to say the same thing. Relax, give, loosen, softly flex. It is all the same. To trigger a left turn with soft weight-shift I let go of all muscle tension in my left foot and leg. To trigger a turn to the right, I relax my right foot and leg. And on and on, down and down, a virtually effortless approach to starting turns..

And perhaps you have also noticed that I am really just talking about starting, or triggering turns, because—as we have already learned—once a turn starts, it keeps on arcing around by itself as long as we stay balanced over that turning outside ski. Start the turn and enjoy the ride. And that's it. *The biggest secret of soft skiing: soft weight-shift through relaxation.*

The Importance of Long Turns

Okay, these new turns with soft weight-shift are great, most likely easier, more fluid and effortless than anything yet. But you can't help thinking: there's more to skiing than just these lazy effortless big turns on moderately easy slopes. You're right. To ski the whole mountain, any mountain, you need a whole quiver full of turns: Long and lazy, medium, and certainly at least a few short turns for tighter trails, plus some tricks for new snow and powder... Don't worry, we're going to fill in all those blanks, but I wanted to start with what I consider the most basic move in *soft skiing*—the long-radius turn.

That is quite an assertion and I think it deserves a bit of explanation. If you are reading this book, chances are you have already spent quite a bit of time on the ski slopes. You have a pretty good idea of the many varieties of the skiing experience. You know what a big difference there is between a wide-open groomed "green" or "blue" ski run, a friendly "groomer" as we sometimes call it, and a steep, narrow, gnarly "double black diamond" run. Intuitively you probably feel that long turns are okay on easy terrain because on a gentle slope you won't ever go too fast; but you sense that if you were to try some big long turns on a very steep slope you would quickly accelerate out of control. And it's possible that you would. At any rate that is a common perception. But there is an interesting and nearly universal confusion at work when most skiers think about skiing under control. Of course, controlling one's speed down the mountain is basic. And it is commonly assumed that what controls a skier's speed is how hard, or how short one turns. But as the song goes "it ain't necessarily so."

The secret of really effective speed control is indeed turning, not how hard one turns, but rather how far one turns. How far around the turn's arc you go. I'm going to spend a little time with this thought because it is going to allow you to use our easy big long-radius turns on a much greater range of slopes. So bear with me.

Imagine any ski turn as part of a large round arc, drawn by some sort of magical compass on the snow. Now think about what your skis are doing as they follow that arc around on the snow. At the top of the turn, the start of the turn, your skis are actually moving almost horizontally. In the first part of the turn as your skis head down the hill they are sliding down an ever steeper angle. Then, in the fall line (as skiers put it) when you are aimed straight down the hill, the snow underfoot, under your skis, has its maximum angle, the true angle of the slope. But it doesn't stop there. As your skis continue around that arc, the effective angle of the slope beneath them decreases, less and less, until at the bottom of that arc your skis are once more moving horizontally across the hill. And if you just keep on turning, keep on following that arc on the snow, you will actually wind up skiing uphill. And we know what that means—as the angle of the slope underfoot decreases your skis slow down. Eventually, if you follow that arc on around, up the hill, you will ski to a stop. Without any braking on your part. It is the shape of the turn, the shape of the hill, not the force of your turning effort that slows you down, and eventually, if you keep turning long enough, brings you to a dead stop. (If the images in this paragraph seem confusing it's because this concept is devilishly tricky to put into words.)

But this pattern is so very important that I am going to repeat the conclusion once more. *Expert skiers slow down not by turning harder, but by turning farther*—by going farther around the arc of their more-or-less round turns than most intermediate skiers ever do. Let me say this in another way. Many skiers, average skiers, tend to use a pretty crude method for slowing down, for putting on the brakes. They turn their skis sideways across their direction of movement and dig in, scraping the snow, to scrub off speed. But if you look carefully at what the skis of experts are doing as they flow down the mountain, you'll see that their skis are mostly moving forward, arcing forward, not skidding sideways in their turns. You will also see that expert skiers tend to ride their skis around more of the arc than less skilled skiers do—as though they were trying to stretch the turn out and make it last. Experts rely on the path of their turns, the shape of their turns, to control their speed, not the force of their turns. And you can too.

You can tune in to this pattern by progressively, from time to time, selecting ever steeper slopes on which to practice your long turns. You will develop a new relation to speed and speed-control. The feeling of these long radius turns on moderate slopes (not super steep walls, please) is an alternating sensation of speeding up, then slowing down, speeding up again then slowing down again. Acceleration as you ride your skis downhill toward the fall line, then deceleration as those skis arc around onto 'virtually' gentler terrain in the second half of each turn. Get used to this sensation of speeding up and then slowing back down in each turn. The slowing down part, the second half of your turns, should be smooth and progressive. Never jerky and quick.

For all too many average intermediate skiers, on anything but the flattest slope, turns seem more of a crisis than a delicious experience. It has to do with that sense of acceleration, and the nagging suspicion that one's skis may just keep on accelerating, faster and faster from one turn to the next, until the inevitable crash. This case of turn-acceleration anxiety is more or less subliminal, or subconscious. But it's often there, and skiers respond to it by cutting the turn short, by twisting their skis quickly around to the opposite direction. The dreaded twist-skid pattern that is so prevalent on the slopes everywhere. And frankly, aside from the smooth way that big turns slow you down, big long-radius turns just feel wonderful. They are expansive, open, free. Expressions like swooping, flying and soaring come to mind. A long series of big round turns feels unhurried; time is on your side; you breathe more easily; you can actually notice the beautiful landscape you are skiing through. Long turns, and especially linked long turns, where the end of one big arc blends smoothly and seamlessly into the next, are totally addictive. This is simply a more graceful, more relaxing way to ski. And hasn't that been our goal all along?

By practicing your soft long-radius turns on progressively more serious slopes, you will quickly develop a new sense of what skiing under control, or more specifically, what speed-control, is all about. Keep turning, stay comfortably balanced over that outside ski, keep arcing around, and you are going to slow down. Period. I want to suggest that you let this become your basic way of slowing down, or even stopping at the end of a good run. Arcing around in as big a circle as you have room for. Not flipping your skis sideways and scraping to a stop. Reinforce your developing big-turn habit as much as you can.

Long Turns – Yes
But Not Only Long Turns

Of course there's more. As I said a few pages ago, you are going to need a variety of turns to ski the whole mountain. A long-radius turn where your outside ski seems to follow its own side curve, on its own, may well become the "home base" move of your skiing, but you are going to need to shorten that turn too. You need medium turns, turns of all different sizes, and eventually you will develop a beautiful short turn too. So how do we do this?

To tighten up the radius of your turns, you are going to concentrate on the second half of each turn. You'll remember that our basic recipe for the soft weight-shift that starts us turning is subtle but complete relaxation of the muscles in your downhill foot and leg. Your downhill side (from the snow up) "gives," gets loose, as though it was gently, invisibly collapsing. Your uphill foot and leg take up the slack, so to speak, supporting you as the top ski starts to roll over to its new edge, and begins to bend, begins to turn. Notice how I am chosing my words to describe something slow and progressive, not sudden and violent. This slow progressive start to each turn is the hallmark of *soft skiing*. Our skis peel off progressively into each new turn; we don't want to pivot them suddenly toward a new turn. So returning back to our topic, how to make shorter turns, let me offer a one-sentence description of the kind of shorter turn we are after: *An effective short turn is actually a long-radius turn that gets tightened up as it progresses*. Does that make sense? I hope so. I am not just playing with words when I say that a good short turn is actually a good long turn that gets shortened up *after* it starts. But it absolutely needs to start slowly and smoothly just like all the big turns we have been triggering with our soft weight-shift.

So there is only one more question to answer here: what exactly do you, the skier, need to do to tighten up that long turn once it's started? That's easy. Just try turning your outside foot a little inside its boot. What? Can it be that simple? Well, yes. Here is a closer look.

It turns out that whenever you want your skis to do something special, anything special, you can give them a subtle but real signal with your foot, inside your ski boot. It makes sense. Your foot is the closest part of your body to the ski and the snow. Most of the time you are standing, well balanced, in the middle of your boot. Your weight evenly distributed between the heel and the ball of your foot. Whatever you want the ski to do on the snow, you make that move with your foot inside your boot. For example, if you need to edge your skis more than normal (for example, to traverse across an icy patch on the mountain) you are simply going to "edge" your foot inside your boot, and that's it. So it makes sense that if you want a turning ski to turn a little faster, you only have to nudge it in a turning sense, with your foot inside your boot. Apply a little turning pressure with your foot in the boot, and what happens? The tip of the ski will bite the snow a little bit more, the tail may slide a little bit more, and the turn you are already arcing will tighten up, or shorten. It should be obvious by now, I hope, that I am talking about the outside foot of a turn, since we have learned that it is the outside ski that is really doing all the work.

Ski technique, like life itself, is not all black and white, all one thing or the other, there are actually dozens of subtle options that skilled skiers can use to fine-tune the radius of their turns. And so I confess that adding a little more turning or steering action with your outside foot (gently applied inside the boot) is not your only option for shortening up your turns. But I think it is probably the easiest and simplest. You can also press a bit forward against the tongue of that outside boot—which will make your ski tips bite a bit more and shorten your turn. Or, almost the same thing, you could flex your legs forward in the direction of your turn (a move that applies both a bit more forward pressure as well as a bit more edge) and your skis will respond by turning faster, shorter.

Shortening the arc of a long turn. Often a slight foot effort inside the boot does the trick. A little forward press of the knees can help too....

Another intriguing way to make your skis turn faster and shorter is an unlikely but very effective action that my friend, the great coach Harald Harb, has called phantom edging. This involves rolling your light inside foot over toward the inside of the turn (for example, rolling your right foot on to its right edge or right side as you make a right turn). It is as though you were trying to increase the natural edge angle of that inside ski. You aren't really increasing its edge bite because that ski stays light, just skimming the surface of the snow. But this phantom edging move has the surprising effect of creating, automatically, a strong edge angle on the weighted outside ski, and—presto—that ski will carve a shorter, snappier turn.

Phantom edging to shorten a turn, a beautiful move but difficult to demonstrate without lifting the light inside ski off the snow.

What a confusion of choices, of possible moves, you are thinking. Yes, it's true. Expert skiers have a lot of options as they play with their skis and subtly fine-tune their turns. It's also true that highly experienced skiers don't actually ever think about what technique to use when. They just ski, in the most relaxed and unselfconscious way, trusting their bodies, and in particular trusting their well trained skiers' legs and feet to do the right thing on their own. I feel that I want my skis to turn faster, to shorten up that arc, and it just seems to happen. Well and good, but how are we going to get you to that point?

The answer is similar to the answer that a visitor to New York is said to have received when he asked: "How do you get to Carneige Hall?" Practice, practice, practice. And that is what we are about to do. That is also why my first suggestion about shortening the arc of your turn involved feeling your feet guide that turn, inside your boots. Your feet do it all. They are the closest part of your body to your skis. Any movement you make, with any part of your body, has to pass through your feet and boots before it can ever effect your skis. So why not begin there? With the feet? This is not just a ski-technique tip. It is something much more general than that. Remember, at the very beginning of this chapter, I said that a one-sentence over-simplification of expert skiing might be: *experts balance with their hands and they ski with their feet*. It's true and it is time to zero in on this idea. Sensing and practicing how your feet can control the speed or radius of a turn is the perfect opportunity to do so.

Right now, at home reading this book, you can feel what I

am talking about and why it works. I am going to assume you are sitting in a chair, not sprawled out on a sofa. In that seated position, place your feet solidly on the floor (not dangling beneath the chair). Wiggle your toes or thump your heels or something like that, just to feel, really feel, where your feet are at this moment. Now, take your right foot and start to twist it slowly to the left. Not pivoting the foot to the left from the heel. But instead, putting a bit of pressure on the ball of that right foot, just behind your big toe while you twist your foot to the left (naturally feeling the heel of that foot swing slightly out to the right). It may take a few tries to get it and feel what I am talking about, but this is the action that goes on, subtly, invisibly, in your boot as you guide your turning ski into a tighter arc. There is a very slight increase in muscle tension as you pivot your right foot to the left with some pressure on the ball of the foot. Did you feel it? Good. If not, don't worry, you will. Try this mini exercise on both sides: twisting your right foot to the left, and your left foot to the right. And then, next time you find yourself cruising down a wide open slope with those graceful slow-to-start long-radius turns we have been practicing, I want you to try to rediscover that feeling of turning your feet, patiently, inside your boots. Sure enough, a little extra steering/guiding/twisting effort inside your boot is all you need to tighten the arc of a lazy big turn. For the technically minded, I should explain that this subtle foot action inside your boot is putting more pressure on the front edge of your outside ski (a little bit is all that's needed) and the ski's tendency to keep turning is enhanced and increased.

Voila—shorter turns. As promised.

Now you can play with the shape of your turns. And friends, watching you glide down the slope won't have a clue what you are doing to make your skis turn faster, tighter, or conversely longer and looser. But remember, a good ski turn starts slowly and progressively. We want to make our turns shorter by tightening up the second half of the arc. Not by twisiting suddenly and more vigorously at the start. OK? And one last reminder, I am talking about shorter turns, long-radius arcs becoming medium-radius arcs. Not really short, really tight turns. Not those tack-tack-tack, windshield-wiper, back-and-forth tight turns that experts sometimes need to negotiate really narrow spots. These tightly linked short-radius turns will come later, and for that we will need to learn one more new trick, anticipation. But not yet…

Relax goddammit!
Learning to Let Go

We've already come a long way. Your patience has paid off. More than once I have asked you to restrict your serious practicing to rather easy slopes: groomed of course, not too steep, wide open. Inviting white playgrounds where you really don't need to turn at all, or hardly need to turn. Where you can practice the gentle art of *soft skiing* without any concerns about going too fast, losing control and crashing. This is a very good strategy for practicing new moves but it's hardly a recipe for skiing the whole mountain. Now, with your soft weight-shift starting to feel almost second nature, with dozens, perhaps hundreds and hundreds of beautiful long turns behind us, it is time to find out what happens when the mountain gets more challenging, as it always does.

Steep slopes are scary, at least they can be. And what do we do when we get scared? All of us, me as well as you. Why, we tense up of course. That's the rub. Because the secret of *soft skiing*, as we have seen, is to relax, to let go. That's how we start our turns, by relaxing one foot and leg. And that's how we stay poised and balanced over our turning skis, waiting for them to finish the job, instead of tensing up and twisting them around. This is where the average skier faces a real dilemma. Because as slopes get steeper and more challenging, one needs to relax even more, to exaggerate that "give," that "loosening up," that folding/collapsing/letting go of the downhill leg which triggers a smooth start to our turns. But the natural reaction to increased steepness, to increased challenge is to tighten up. Dang! And it gets worse. Because the harder you try to relax, the less relaxed you become. And the tenser you become, the harder each turn seems. Your balance and your confidence, as well as your technique go all to hell. And please don't think that this paradox, this dilemma, is something that only intermediate or average skiers have to deal with. It affects us all. It's simply that after years of expert skiing my threshold of nervousness, for example, is very high. I don't get nervous and tense on slopes that might freak out my ski students. But yes, my comfort zone has very real limits. I've also learned a number of ways to defuse this steep-slope anxiety, and come back to my home base mode of relaxed *soft skiing*, no matter how hard or off-putting the slope seems.

The first trick, and the most important one, is to notch up the challenge bit by bit, one step at a time, to take your new *soft skiing* skills to progressively harder slopes but avoid jumping into the deep end of the pool. I used the term "scary" when I mentioned steep slopes, but it's less of a question of actual fear than of simple anxiety. Am I ready? Can I handle it? Will this work? Will it be comfortable? Not: Will I crash and burn? Will I die? So don't go looking for black slopes if you have only been practicing on green ones. Ski the next hardest slope, and the next, and then the next… Don't rush it.

I have equated steepness with difficulty and in a way that's true, although there are other challenges. But to stick with steepness for a moment, I would suggest that as you slowly look for steeper slopes to test your technique, you should avoid really long steep slopes. A short steep pitch is much more reassuring. Yes, it's a bit steep for a couple of turns, but there's the bottom of the slope, a flat trail, a catwalk, whatever, a few moments of challenge and then relax. It's a variation on our familiar theme of picking a slope that will help us perform, not put us off.

And here's another trick for building the confidence that will allow you to relax. Play with the relative speed of your runs. By this I mean ski a bit faster, or maybe quite a bit faster than you usually do in situations that seem very, very easy, trivially easy. Really push your speed where you feel totally confident. Then when you do arrive at a seriously steeper, more challenging slope, you simply slow way down, and it will seem as though you have a lot of extra time to solve whatever problems that slope poses. You will feel calm and confident simply because you will be moving over the snow much more slowly than you have been.

So much for the psychology of staying loose and relaxed, but how about the muscular, kinesthetic side of it all? Do you need to modify your moves, subtle though they are, to use my soft skiing pattern on steeper slopes? Or to put it differently, does relaxing the muscle tension in your downhill foot and leg to start a turn work just the same on a steep slope as on an open cruiser? Not entirely. Here is a variation for starting your turns that I'd like you to play with on steeper slopes. A two part variation. The first part involves getting a little support, a little extra steadiness from your downhill pole. So far I really haven't mentioned your ski poles, for good reason. In cruising skiing, moving gracefully from one long-radius turn to another, your poles and what you do or don't do with them aren't very important. There's a common almost universal tendency to tap the snow with your pole to more or less mark the point at which you start a turn. This pole tap (sometimes called a pole plant) has been a formal part of all ski instruction forever. If you use your pole that way, fine. If not, that's also fine. Using your pole at the start of a turn is only important on steeper slopes, or in very short linked turns (which we haven't tackled yet). But here we are now on a steep but fairly short practice slope, ready to focus on polishing up the start of our turns. At the very moment you want to start a turn down the hill, reach downhill to the side, tap your downhill pole into the snow and—ever so slightly—support yourself on it for an instant. That's all. You may or may not feel this momentary support, no matter, it will slowly develop into something more as you get more comfortable on somewhat steeper slopes.

But the crux of the matter is that business of taking the pressure off your downhill ski, allowing the upper ski to tilt over, bite and lead the turn. On gentle slopes we have focused on relaxing your lower foot and leg, starting with the foot. Now, on somewhat steeper slopes, let that relaxing morph into a real collapsing-folding of that lower leg. It almost feels as though it is flexing out of the way, downhill, in the direction of the coming turn. Once again, start by just thinking about this, imagining it. Don't try to force it. Let it happen. It will.

As you let your downhill leg flex-fold-collapse out of the way, toward the turn, your uphill ski and leg will start the turn, automatically. And yes, this turn will start a little faster than usual. Which is appropriate for a steeper slope where you don't want to linger in the fall line gathering excess speed. But still, these somewhat shorter turns on somewhat steeper slopes, are not jerky tight corners. You don't try to twist the skis around. If you need to shorten these turns, shorten the end of the turn by foot steering, or flexing forward into the end of that arc, as we talked about a few pages back. As you get comfortable with this folding-flexing action of your downhill leg to start steeper turns, you will also start to appreciate that moment of extra support from your downhill pole. It is an "iffy" moment that takes a little getting used to. What I am talking about is letting the support of your downhill ski, foot and leg suddenly vanish. You will feel yourself sinking or "falling" downhill ("falling" is just a way of putting it, you don't of course fall; perhaps "tilting" would be more accurate). It is a sensation that combines giving, or slumping, or somewhat collapsing a bit toward your downhill side. The operative term here is "a bit" or "somewhat." A subtle feeling, a good one to discover. And in essence this folding downhill is a physical, kinesthetic equivalent of relaxing your downhill side. Really relaxing. As you play with the physical part, the mental part, the mental relaxation or letting go at the start of the turn will develop too. You can't make it happen, or force it to happen. But you can coax it into happening... Try it.

Skiing With the Mountain
Playing with the terrain

You have probably already spotted something a bit artificial with my suggested patterns for mastering *soft skiing*. At first I encouraged you to chose and to use wide-open, gentle, groomed green slopes. A few minutes ago, I was talking about selecting steep but short pitches to practice on. Yet real ski mountains are more than just flat or just steep. The terrain of a skier's winter playground is almost infinitely variable. Few slopes are smooth geometric planes. Some snowy pitches are slightly concave, others convex. There are not only bump slopes formed by hundreds of skiers turning on the same spots, but natural bumps and rolls, rises and hollows, fall-away slopes, gullies, forested stands too dense to penetrate on skis, and slopes with wide-spaced tree trunks that seem inviting, open and friendly. All this variety in skiing terrain

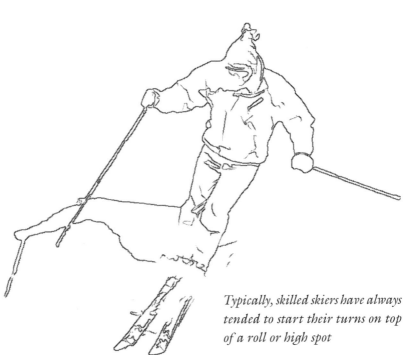

Typically, skilled skiers have always tended to start their turns on top of a roll or high spot

adds up to a pleasure park not an obstacle course.

There is a tendency in teaching skiing, or in writing about skiing, to present a turn as if it were a platonic ideal. The perfect turn. The perfect turn that you want to master, and then repeat, and repeat endlessly. Every weekend. Down every slope. I'm as guilty as anyone of this kind of oversimplification. But like the lyrics from Porgy and Bess, "it ain't necessarily so." For someone who delights in the ease of *soft skiing*, a perfect run is probably one in which no two turns are the same. Sometimes when the slope opens up you feel like opening up your turns, stretching them out, using up all the white space before you with longer and longer turns. Sometimes you arrive at an area that seems crowded with skiers, without thinking you slow down, you shorten your turns, you weave in and around. Sometimes the slope is so well groomed that there is really no difference between starting a turn here, or here, or here. But on other slopes it seems obvious, inevitable that this roll, this change in slope, this particular spot is the ideal place to start a turn.

Typically, skilled skiers have always tended to start their turns on top of a roll or high spot, or some kind of hump in the snow. Why? In earlier days with much stiffer skis, people were preoccupied with the need to get their body weight momentarily off their skis, to make them light in order to turn them. This so-called "unweighting" was the basis of all ski instruction for generations. And that is why skiers have traditionally tended to start their turns on a high point in the slope, whether a small bump, or large roll in the terrain. Because as you ski over such a high point, the fact that the ground is "dropping away" on the other side makes your skis lighter, a kind of automatic unweighting from the shape of the terrain. But today unweightng is no longer needed in order to start a turn. In fact it's almost the opposite. Shifting your weight off the lower ski to stand on the uphill ski as it rolls over and starts a turn is really a form of pre-weighting that new outside ski. But skiers still like to start their turns on top of rolls and humps in the snow, or breaks where the slope drops away. And why is that? Because it feels so good. It's that same sense of lightness, of floating, and yes, of weighing less if only for a brief moment. This terrain unweighting

from turning on a high point used to be important, now it's just a pleasant sensation. So I suggest you play with this idea of using various different points on the hill to start your turns. Expand your horizons by consciously varying your path down the slope. I've already put my finger on large long-radius turns as representing the essence of soft skiing, and they do. But in that range there are endless variations. Try letting the shape of the hill, and all its smaller mini-shapes and undulations guide your skiing responses. Your goal, easier to realize than you might guess, is to ski with the mountain not against it. If the shape of the hill in front of you suggests a certain path, accept that suggestion and see where it leads.

This is where you begin to say goodbye to ski technique.

Because the goal of learning any technique, especially these simple lessons of *soft skiing*, is to then to forget them, and just ski. Spontaneously. Without thinking. Just soaking in the pleasure of a winter day, of graceful motion, of the freedom to fly down a mountain without working. And if you have followed me so far, I'd say you are almost there.

Do we ever become perfect, and perfectly accomplished skiers?

Part III

Soft Skiing Down Harder Slopes
Expanding your Horizons
& Pushing your Limits

Congratulations. You look good on skis, and what's more important, you feel good. Some days, some runs, you feel completely at one with your skis, at one with the mountain. Soft weight shift has become a habit, a comfortable, trusted habit. Some days, it almost seems you are communicating with your skis by a kind of mental telepathy. You think about arcing to the right, and voila, your are doing it. Your right foot relaxes, softens and progressively your left ski starts to bite and bend, peeling off in perfect arc, a perfect long-radius turn. You cruise down the mountain, almost any mountain, in delicious long smooth arcs, enjoying the ride, enjoying the view.

Not only that, when you feel like tightening up those turns, you can do so, almost without trying, certainly without thinking, a little more steering action with that outside foot, a little more gentle flexing into your arc, and those shorter turns, one after the other, just happen. You are skiing as though it is the most natural thing you have ever done. As though you were born skiing. As though you have been skiing all your life, and today, you never once thought about how you do it. It feels so natural.

You've arrived, you're there.

But are we really ever there? Do we ever become perfect, and perfectly accomplished skiers? Or do these snow-covered mountains always reserve more surprises, more delights, and in particular, more challenges for us? Of course they do.

Some challenges are obvious, and obviously not appealing to every skier. Especially not to the relaxed older skier who has been my target audience in this book. Not to me either. At this point in my skiing life I am not going to jump off cornices into steep and icy chutes. I am not going to look at the trail map when I visit a new ski mountain and try to figure out the hardest trail for my very first run — although with a young skier's rashness I might have done exactly that thirty years ago. No, sticking with my goal of graceful effortless elegant skiing, *soft skiing*, I am definitely not going to beat myself up looking for major athletic and psychological challenges. And I suspect you aren't going to either. But we can still expand our skiing horizons without turning our back on the key notions of *soft skiing*, letting our skis, and the mountain, and gravity do all the work. While we enjoying the ride. If I can do this, believe me, you can too.

So this section is going to explore further challenges, optional challenges: steeper slopes, deeper snow, and not merely very deep powder but also strange, awkward, difficult snow conditions (yes they happen). You can think of this whole part of our shared ski learning adventure as the graduate course, the extra-credit part of the course. You are already good. How can you get better? How can you ski and enjoy slopes harder than the ones you enjoy today? How can you, if the mood strikes you, look for new skiing challenges, and meet them in the spirit and style of *soft skiing*?

That's an important question because if we are not careful here we will wander off in search of each and every possible expert skill to solve each and every possible expert skiing problem. I did that already in my book, *Breakthrough on the New Skis*, which is still in print and really does deliver the secrets of surviving, mastering and learning to love some of the toughest challenges the mountain can offer. And no, soft skiing doesn't work everywhere, on every slope, in every possible snow condition…

Take bump skiing or mogul skiing. I don't have to tell you that bump skiing is hard. Everyone knows that. And as a matter of fact, it is actually possible to ski bumps in a soft, relaxed and fluid way. But not only does that take a lot of time and practice, it almost certainly entails some very awkward moments, some hard thumps, and doubtless a few good crashes. Not only aren't bumps themselves easy, but neither is a bump skiing apprenticeship. Since I have targeted this book on *Soft Skiing* toward older skiers, I am pretty sure that most of my readers aren't waiting breathlessly for a bump lesson. So I am going to skip this particular challenge in this book. If you're tempted to make your peace with moguls, I am going to recommend that you read the bump chapter in my *Breakthrough on the New Skis* book, and watch my video, *Bumps and Powder Simplified*.*

---

*Both my book, *Breakthrough on the New Skis*, and all my *Breakthrough on Skis* videos are available on-line, at www.amazon.com or at my own skiing web site, www.breakthroughonskis.com

What I do hope to achieve in this section is to open the door to using your *soft-skiing* skills on steeper slopes, in powder and deep snow, and even in lousy snow and occasionally on icy slopes (brrrr…). Lets get started.

Steeper and Steeper

How do expert skiers cope with ever steeper slopes? The answer is deceptively simple: with ever shorter turns.

Earlier generations of skiers really made a fetish out of very short linked turns, straight down the hill, down the fall line as we say. "Short swing" is the proper ski-jargon term for this tack-tack-tack, or sometimes swish-swish-swish, back-and-forth, back-and-forth, back-and-forth dance down the fall line. Every alpine country gives it a special name: *Wedeln* in Austria, *godille* in France and most evocative, *serpentina* in Italy. Nowadays, however, skiers are much more relaxed about linked short turns: they are simply something you use when you need to rather than a maneuver for showing off what an accomplished skier you are. But it's still true that the ability to turn, turn, turn, in tight continuous arcs, straight down the hill, is one of the hallmarks of real expertise on skis.

Very short turns depend on *anticipation*, a much used, much abused and much misunderstood term in the world of ski technique. Originally "anticipation" meant that if a skier was more or less facing down the hill, at the very start of a short turn, then that skier was "anticipating" what his or her skis were about to do. And sure enough, when we watch a very skilled skier come straight down the hill in a series of short, short turns, it looks as though that skier's body isn't moving, isn't turning at all, but that only the skis are turning back and forth beneath the skier. A nice image and an accurate one. Because anticipation is much more than simply aiming your upper body down the hill, in the direction of the coming turn, before releasing your skis to follow. (Even though that is more or less the way it was described in the seminal book by George Joubert from which I learned to ski, way, way back in 1965). Turning your upper body down the hill seems to me to be a very static view of anticipation. The modern view of anticipation—dynamic anticipation—and the way I have been teaching it for years, involves continuous motion, continuous turning, action then reaction, each turn triggering or provoking the turn back in the opposite direction. Anticipation describes a skiing pattern where the end of one turn sets you up for the start of the next one, actually makes the next turn happen, or at least makes it easy.

This is a tricky concept, so I hope you will bear with me as I try to paint a verbal picture of this ingenious and subtle way of linking short turns. It works something like this: a skier's upper body or trunk is relatively large and stable compared to the a skier's legs and feet. So when the time comes for short turns, there is a sense of twisting and steering one's legs and skis against the quiet mass of one's upper body. This more rapid steering/guiding action of your legs and feet tends to "wind the skis up" beneath you, and then—when the turn is over and you "let go"—your skis unwind beneath you, pivoting back down the hill into the next turn. Thus skiing with anticipation is a kind of pendulum action, back and forth, side to side, winding up then unwinding back down the hill, turn and re-turn, turn and re-turn. It is as though a short turn in one direction creates an equal but opposite turn back in the other direction. Indeed it does. But saying this, painting this word-picture of skis turning back and forth beneath a quiet almost motionless upper body is not the same as teaching you how to do it. How can you make this pattern of turn and re-turn, action and re-action, your own?

The first step is to really loosen up and relax. Sound familiar? Yes, but here I am talking about relaxing your hips and lower back so that your legs can rotate and move easily beneath your hips and torso, without causing your torso to move. A kind of disconnecting or uncoupling of your torso from your legs. A good way of feeling and practicing this upper-lower body independence is with what we call a hockey stop. Hockey stops are simply a way of sliding to a stop, by pivoting your skis sideways and scraping along the snow, without letting your upper body turn too. Try this near the bottom of a comfortable slope. And trigger your hockey stop with a sort of sinking, slumping relaxation, at the same time turning your feet and skis sideways, but not digging in to the slope. It is important to slide to a stop, letting your skis brush across the slope. I repeat: brush the slope.

Do you remember when I described how skis turn (back in the beginning of **Part II, Your Story**)? I described two very different turning principles built in to our skis. One was the "carved turn" principle and the other was the "slipped or

Hockey Stops, your feet turn and slide,
your body doesn't turn. A neat trick

skidded turn" principle. I mentioned that very few turns are all
skid, or all carve, and that usually there is a bit of both going
on at the same time. Well, as our turns get shorter and shorter,
inevitably we will experience more slipping or skidding, and less
carving. It is important to realize this, observe it, let it happen,
and accept it. Even embrace this extra slipping of the skis over
the snow as a key advantage in short turns. Many skiers, once
they have experienced the delicious sensation of carving turns,
are tempted to make too big a deal about carving. Some almost
make a religion of carving and feel bad when they can't carve

every turn. Now it's true that the big, long-radius turns we focused on earlier are naturally going to be much more carved. But as you make shorter turns, and especially when practicing a few hockey stops, it's the opposite. In shorter turns, try to keep your feet relaxed inside your boots and let your skis slip across the snow. Your skis will come around all the more quickly.

Sideslipping used to be a key building block of any skier's skill set. Nowadays, however, a lot of skiers have never really learned, consciously and formally, to sideslip. And most have never practiced it. I am not suggesting that you go out and find a short smooth steep pitch and practice sideslipping. But I will suggest that you become more aware of it as you decide to tackle steeper slopes. If you are standing with your feet and skis pointed across the hill, you will stay there, or track forward, but not slide sideways down the hill, as long as the edges of your skis bite the snow. And what makes those edges bite? A certain amount of muscle tension in your feet. When you tighten your feet in your boots, your skis will grip better, edge better. In an earlier day, ski instructors talked a lot about edging with knees and hips, but I reckon all edging action starts down at the foot level. It may sound a bit vague just to say "to edge tighten your feet in your boots" but the sensation is actually as though you were trying to lift the outside edge of your foot and perhaps the toes of the foot, upwards in the boot. That takes muscle tension in the foot, and that is precisely what makes your skis edge strongly. Relax your foot, let it go soft, and you will feel your skis begin to slip down the hill, to brush over the snow.

That's sideslipping. Sideslippping can gently ease you down a pitch that might seem too steep for a comfortable turn. Or a bit of slipping can make your short turns even shorter. When a ski is strongly edged it wants to follow the long curve of its side cut. And a long-radius turn results. But without strong edging, your skis can arc or brush or smear around in a much shorter turn... Try it. We already learned about relaxing the muscle tension on one side, in one foot, as a way of shifting weight to the other foot and ski. Now, as you play around with short and shorter turns, just try to let your feet stay loose and soft inside

Short turns from above: the skis turn, the body doesn't. Short turns are easier without much edging; so let'em slide

your boots. Your short short turns will improve.

What else can you do to facilitate, and polish, and smooth out your short turns? Don't forget to use your poles. I have scarcely mentioned poles so far in this book. Truth is that pole action is not very important, maybe not important at all, in long slow turns. But as you shorten your turns, a steady tap, tap, tap with your poles—once for each turn—can help maintain a rhythm, and give you an extra sense of security on steeper slopes. This taping or planting of the downhill pole, just before turning has a few other advantages in terms of short turns. Reaching down the hill toward the next turn effectively keeps your body from swinging around the corner each time you turn. Remember that image of the skiers body moving straight down the hill while skis and legs turn back and forth without seeming to turn the skier's upper body. Well, reaching straight down the hill and planting your pole before each turn tends to reinforce that pattern. It can eliminate even a split second of hesitation as you shift to the new top or outside ski, commit your body and start the turn. And on the steepest of slopes your downhill pole, planted straight down the hill below you, really does give you a sense of extra support in that "wobbly moment" when you let your strong downhill leg collapse, or "give," or "fold" into the new turn. In cruising skiing, poles have almost no real technical function. But making short turns on steep slopes, they can become your best friends…

Still, the perceptive reader of this book (and I hope you are all perceptive readers) may be thinking right now: Lito is painiting a good picture of how skiers link short turns with anticipation, but he hasn't really presented a step-by-step method for learning to do it. That is sort of true, and it isn't an accident. My primary goal in writing *Soft Skiing*, has been to open the door to a gentle style of cruising down open slopes with effortless big turns. In this section I only wanted to sketch out a few other options for those moments when cruising, and simply "letting go" and riding your skis' natural arc doesn't seem too good an option. Once again, it is time to mention that in my book, *Breakthrough On The New Skis*, I go into more detail, describing these more challenging situations, and teaching the best techniques to handle them. If you are really motivated to master short turns straight down the fall line, on ever steeper slopes, that book can be your secret weapon. Now, lets look at something that is a lot more fun, deep snow and powder

Deeper and Deeper

There is a wonderful mystique associated with skiing powder, deep powder. For skiers powder skiing has always been a kind of achievable ultimate. First tracks down a fresh slope of untracked snow represnt a sort of skier's Holy Grail. But somehow, not for everyone. Dyed-in-the wool powder skiers, those happy few who have figured out how to ski powder, claim there is nothing better. Those who haven't yet made their peace with powder feel frustrated and betrayed when their weekend ski trip is "spoiled" by a foot or more of fresh snow. And there is also the matter of what I have always called "the powder paradox." Once you

*First tracks down a fresh slope of untracked snow represent
a sort of skier's Holy Grail.*

have learned how to ski in untracked snow, deep snow, powder snow, it seems and in fact it is significantly easier than skiing on a packed slope. But on the other hand, it's harder to learn to ski powder than to learn solid technique for packed slopes.

At least it used to be. After mastering the subtleties of foot-to-foot skiing, of soft weight shift, of trusting your outside ski to bring you around the arc of your turn, suddenly everything seems to change. In really deep snow, if you get all your weight on one foot, one ski, you're in trouble. Because in really deep snow one weighted ski will dive beneath the surface, while the light ski floats up. And the hapless skier struggles to maintain balance on two skis going in opposite directions. So traditionally, skiers had to unlearn weight shift in order to ski powder successfully. And they needed to build a set of new skiing habits—standing equally on both skis, so that both skis would float equally in this new 3D medium of deep snow. It worked, but it wasn't easy. At least until the introduction of short fat powder skis. These skis changed everything. That long and frustrating powder skiers apprenticeship was cut short. And somehow, with these new 7-league skis, shorter but above all much fatter than normal skis, people who had never been able to cope with deep snow found themselves handling it with no problem. Not just handling it but falling in love with it. And that's the short version of what I am about to share with you. If your want to ski powder, and enjoy it, get yourself a pair of fat powder skis. Buy them, rent them, beg, borrow or steal them (only kidding) but fat powder skis will change your life, I promise. Let's look closer.

Actually, I do recommend that you rent a pair of fat powder skis the next time you find yourself at a ski area facing an overnight dump of more than just a few inches of fresh snow. That's the ideal way to start the process of becoming a fanatic powder skier. These skis will look a bit funny when you take them out of the rental shop, or look down at them on your feet during the day's first chairlift ride. But they won't feel funny when you head off into untracked snow. Here is why, and here's what they do. The secret is flotation. The extra surface area of a very wide or very fat ski is going to float you up in the deep snow, even when you have all your weight on one ski. They don't dive into the deep stuff, stall and topple you over. In deep snow fat skis are totally forgiving. Just ski. You can make every "mistake" in the book, and you probably won't fall. In fact you will probably feel great. This doesn't mean that with a more polished powder technique you won't enjoy the deep snow even more. So here is how to get there.

Real comfort in deep snow is more than anything a matter of balance and stability. You need to become comfortable even though you are no longer standing on a solid surface of packed snow, but instead, floating on a snowy pillow of variable thickness and softness. So I suggest you begin your powder adventure by going straight. Terrain permitting of course. Just pick a straight line, steep enough to keep moving, but not steep enough to scare you, and get used to the powder by simply streaking through it. You will be developing your powder skiers balance and stance. Try to stand equally on both feet, both skis, and to help yourself

do this, you can try bouncing or flexing a little as you simply glide through the powder. And why not? Try spreading your arms a little more than normal to the side for even better lateral balance. You will also discover something about the natural speed control effect of deep snow or powder. You are no longer skiing on the snow, but in it. And so you encounter more resistance than normal. So much snow slows you down. That is why skilled skiers generally pick a steeper line down the mountain in deep snow than they do on the pack. Speed is your friend in deep snow. Speed will help you plow through that extra resistance and it will also cause your skis to float upwards in the snow, toward the top of the new powder.

But however useful cutting straight across fields of fresh snow might be in developing a powder stance and a powder-skier's sense of balance on both skis, it doesn't come close to those long sinuous esses, those smooth linked turns, that are the greatest pleasure in untracked snow. And anyway, one needs to turn to navigate a path to the bottom of the mountain. So let's turn our attention to the turn. What's different, what's the same in deep snow? Surprisingly our soft-skiing focus on long turns, on smooth progressive starts to those turns, on not twisting our skis violently in a new direction will all pay off when we enter the realm of deep snow. If you twist your skis violently at the start of a turn on a packed slope you will simply make a bad turn. But if you try that in deep snow, your skis will doubtless catch in the snow, and you will tumble. So your turns in powder need to start slowly, and continue slowly. When you are riding up the lift, look at the tracks skilled powder skiers leave in fresh snow. They are stretched out, sinuous, there are no sudden changes of direction… You want to ski powder like that.

Something else will get your attention as you begin to explore powder on your fat skis, a sensation of skiing in slow motion. Everything takes longer because of the resistance of the soft snow all around your skis. Let go. Let it happen. Your skis will slowly come around in the deep stuff. You won't accelerate like mad. It's a slow motion dance, a gentle lyrical waltz, not a boogie. And finally, maybe I ought to offer a few hints about just how one starts turns in deep snow. I've already implied, and actually said straight out, that weight shift doesn't work in powder. Soft weight shift or any kind of weight shift. (You will remember that shifting to the new outside ski would bend that ski, and the curved edge would bite and bring you around—on the pack that is). But in powder, edges don't play a role in turning. The soft snow is pushing evenly against the whole bottom surface of your ski, of both skis. So all you need to do is start a gentle steering motion with both feet. Twisting, yes, but barely. And as you turn your feet, your skis will bank slightly against the snow, and the push-back of the snow against the slightly banked bottoms of your skis will tend to keep pushing or guiding you into the turn. This sounds complex but it isn't. Pick up enough speed that you feel your skis begin to plane or float in the powder, steer the fronts of your skis into the start of a new turn. And wait! As always, a turn once started tends to keep going. Don't rush it, and when you have come around a fair bit, but before you have lost all your speed, do it again. And again. And again.

Don't forget to smile. You are skiing powder. And if you do everything wrong, your magical fat skis will save you and give you another chance to relax and let it happen...

Weird, tough or challenging conditions.

Skiers have their own vocabulary. For some reason, really bad snow is often called "crud." Crud can be sloppy wet gooey spring snow. It can be breakable crust. It can be day-old powder that isn't powder any more, criss-crossed and cut up by hundreds of tracks and then frozen overnight into lumps that seem determined to get you. Because of remarkable advances in slope grooming techniques and equipment, you can easily spend a whole ski season without ever needing to ski a single run in bad snow, in crud. But it happens. And when it does, those same fat powder skis we talked about earlier are your secret weapon. They will float you over all those lumps, through treacherous crust, across deep spring slush. Trust them. In bad snow, fat skis make you a better and far more secure skier. You don't even need to really understand why (although it comes from that increased surface area and increased floatation). It just happens.

But there is at least one set of tough ski conditions where fat skis won't help. Although I'm not talking about tough snow conditions, because I am not thinking about snow at all. I am thinking about ice. Slopes can get a bit icy, or very icy, or sometimes turn into real sheets of ice. This can be the result of skiers scraping away the soft surface snow on a popular trail when it hasn't snowed for weeks. Or ice can result, in spring, from afternoon melting and overnight freezing. New England ice is legendary. Western ski resorts boast softer fluffier snow, but yes, even Utah resorts, famous for light powder, sometimes see their slopes ice up. However and whenever it happens, ice ain't nice. Suffice it to say, that if most of our skiing experience took place on ice or icy slopes, we wouldn't be such enthusiastic, dedicated skiers. But yes, ice too is skiable. You can make your peace with it. And here are some hot tips for handling icy slopes.

Technically ice is the exact opposite of deep snow or powder. When the mountain is covered in a foot or more of new snow, the challenge is that there is too much resistance. The new snow blocks the easy sliding of our skis which is why we have to let our speed build before starting to turn. But ice puts the skier in a situation where there is not enough resistance to the movement, the sliding of our skis. Yet here too we need to avoid sudden movements and especially over-turning or over-pivoting our skis. If you twist your skis on an icy slope, they tend to spin around underneath you. So subtle smooth soft motion is once again the key. Soft skiing all over again.

Poise and balance—smooth soft motion with no sudden twisting is the key to coping with ice.

On an icy mountain, use some cunning and simply avoid steep slopes. Steep icy slopes are a real headache because they seem to demand short turns, and short turns are an invitation to over-acting, over-pivoting, over-twisting and skittering sideways down the slope. You will of course skid sideways like crazy every time you over-twist or over-initiate a turn on ice. So you will be looking for moderate open slopes, not narrow icy trails. And you will want to find terrain that invites you to make large open gentle turns. They really work on icy slopes. And they take almost no effort to start. A gentle invisible weight-shift, the softest of soft weight shifting and your skis will arc into a new turn. In this sense, ice calls on us to use the absolute minimum of ski technique.

But I can suggest more. Two hot tips for cold icy slopes. The first is to turn against the terrain not with it. By that I mean that I try to launch and guide my turns in the hollow low spots on the slope, not on the high spots, like the tops of swales or rolls in the terrain. Intuitively most skiers have always figured out that it is somehow easier to turn on the high spots. As you pass the top of a roll or hillock on the slope, the snow drops away. Your skis feel lighter and turns happen almost by themselves (although it is true that we don't really need this form of "terrain unweighting" with our modern skis and with effective weight shift). But on icy slopes this very lightening of the skis as you pass the top of a roll tends to make them skid out. Turns are harder to control. If instead you turn in the hollow spots the shape of the hill puts more pressure on your skis, helping your edge to grip the hard icy snow, and minimizing your skis tendency to skid out from under you. Turning in the hollow spots seems counter-intuitive but it works like gangbusters on ice. Try it.

My second tip is to be careful about edging your skis. Too much edge and your skis will slide out and skid rather than hold their line. Again it's paradoxical. More edging, more of an edge angle, does not equal more gripping. So skilled skiers who have developed a sixth sense for coping with ice tend to "feather" the edges of their skis. They edge gently, never suddenly, just enough and no more. There is no way to discover how much effort is too much on ice except through practice, trial and error on icy days. But your goal is clear, to do as little as you need to do, and actually much less than you might imagine. Stay poised and balanced, and ride your skis without ever overpowering them. It's a subtle game, best played on icy slopes that aren't particularly steep. But the satisfaction of handling an icy run well, of arcing down an icy mountain without losing it in a series of awkward scraping sideways skids. That satisfaction is immense. One more sign that you have crossed over into the world of expert skiing. One more demonstration of the efficient beauty of *soft skiing*.

Ice may be nice. but powder is still better....

And with that it's time to end our look at more challenging slopes and ski conditions, our excursion beyond the basics of *soft skiing*, beyond the limits of simply cruising a wide-open winter playground of inviting skier-friendly slopes. Although I must admit that's where my heart is, cruising as an art form, cruising skiing as pure delight.

In one of my Breakthrough-On-Skis instructional videos I quoted a friend's explanation of why he skied: "I'm only in it for the poetry," said John Nesbitt, the author of *Megatrends*. And that goes for me too. That's the ultimate reason that I love *soft skiing*. Skiing without aggression, without fatigue, without effort, but with the mountain, with our great modern skis, with gravity. Challenge is okay, and mountains in winter can provide skiers a lot of challenges if that's what they are looking for, but I'll take the poetry, true poetry in motion, any day. It's my choice. Perhaps it's your choice too.

Enjoy!

Pure motion trumps technique....

Soft skiing in the Alps.

Afterwords

FEEDBACK & FOLLOW UP
MY HOPES FOR THIS BOOK

I wonder if you've enjoyed reading this book as much as I've enjoyed writing it. I hope so. The idea for *Soft Skiing* came from a number of experiences, and a number of skiers. Most of all from a handful of genuinely older skiers, skiers in their 70s and 80s with whom I had the pleasure of skiing during my ten years directing the intensive Breakthrough Ski Weeks program at Aspen and Snowmass. What an inspiration! I wanted to ski like that when I grew up, I told myself (only partially tongue in cheek). And being an ambitious ski teacher, I wanted to be able to teach other older skiers to ski that well too. At some point I realized that my own preferred lazy and energy-efficient style of skiing would be the perfect starting point for such a program. That's where this book comes from.

It's a big order, and as I finish work on this book in the autumn of 2009, I am acutely aware that it could probably be much better if I only had another season or two to test all my ideas, to work on better illustrations, to solicit more help and more feedback about my presentation of *soft skiing*. But knowing that the perfect can be the enemy of the good, I decided to send this first edition out into the ski world, and ask for your feedback and help to make the next edition even better. For sure, there will be a next (revised, improved and added-to) edition. Thanks to the emerging technology of on-demand book printing, it is easier than ever to revise a book and keep it current.

If *Soft Skiing* helped you polish your skiing skills and expand your skiing horizons, let me know. If some of my ideas seemed confusing or hard to put into practice, do let me know. If I forgot to tackle some important aspects of your ski experience, I want to know that too. You can write me at

SoftSkiing@BreakthroughOnSkis.com

And although I travel a lot and may be out-of- pocket for weeks on end, I promise I'll answer all your emails.

As I receive feedback on this book, and this approach to making skiing an easier, more relaxing, more effortless sport, I plan to publish answers to your questions, new insights, tips, addenda and further clarifications of my *soft-skiing* approach on my skiing web site

www.BreakthroughOnSkis.com

I've been editing and producing this web site for over ten years. It's a labor of love and the very best way I know to stay in touch with my many skiing friends. I count you among them, and count on you to spread the word that skiing need not be a "grunt sport" much less the exclusive province of the very young, very energetic and very athletic. Skiing is for all of us. What a gift.

Think snow, and thanks for joining me in this exploration of *soft skiing*!

Lito

Spring snow above Telluride, Colorado.

About the Author

Lito Tejada-Flores was born at 13,000 feet in the Bolivian Andes and since has spent much of his life in high places. He has shared his passion for mountain adventure in a series of books, on wilderness skiing, kayaking and downhill skiing, and in documentary films.

His instructional ski books and videos are well known. But he has also written books on backcountry ski touring and whitewater kayaking. And his documentary film on the ascent of Mount Fitz Roy won the Grand Prize at the International Mountain and Exploration Film Fetival in Trento Italy.

A dedicated, passionate ski instructor for over 30 years, Lito is a mountain-sports and travel writer by profession, a poet by avocation, a graphic designer, web designer, photo editor and documentary filmmaker for the hell of it, and a publisher quite by accident. He has collaborated with his wife and partner, landscape photographer Linde Waidhofer, in designing and publishing a series of award-winning books of western landscape photography under their Western Eye imprint. Their latest collaboration is the book, *This is Skiing, The Impossible Romance of Sliding over Snow.* Today, Lito and Linde spend part of each year in Patagonia and the other part in the Colorado Rockies.

Among Lito's most memorable adventures—first ascents on Mount Fitz Roy in Patagonia and the Devil's Thumb in Alaska... and falling in love with Linde Waidhofer.

OTHER BOOKS & VIDEOS
BY LITO TEJADA-FLORES

This is the book into which I put every single secret I've learned in a lifetime of teaching skiing. Not just a revision of my earlier *Breakthrough on Skis* classic, but a brand-new book, rethought and rewritten from the snow-up so to speak. The chapters on bump skiing and bad snow really demystify and open the door to mastering these classic skiing challenges.

Breakthrough on the New Skis, and all Lito's videos (see the following pages) are available both from *amazon.com* or from Lito's own web site, *www.BreakthroughOnSkis.com.*

Is an image really worth a thousand words? If so this video is priceless. In this one-hour DVD, originally shot on 16mm film by award winning cinematographer Edgar Boyles, Lito covers the essential moves of modern expert skiing. Not a show-off video of ski heroes behaving heroically but rather a patient sequence of achieveable steps and realistic goals—a genuine private lesson that will change your skiing life. Using slow-motion and stop action to underline and clarify the basic moves of expert skiing, Lito covers the whole story: guiding the arc of the turn, a bombproof parallel start, short turns with anticipation. Not just expert skiing simplified but a simplified way to learn, and master, expert skiing.

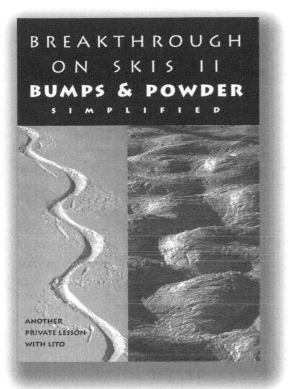

Think of this video as the graduate course. Bumps and powder have always been the biggest challenges for most recreational skiers. This DVD shows you how to treat bumps and powder as old friends. This video is guaranteed to expand your skiing horizons. Bumps and powder will no longer be a struggle, or something to avoid

"No rock music. No big air. Camera angles among the best we've ever seen. Most important, it makes the black art of route finding through bumps easy to understand. The powder section is beautiful to watch, easy to follow, and thoroughly inspiring. You can't help but be inspired."

Bill Grout, senior editor, Skiing magazine

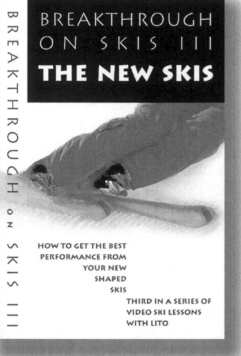

BREAKTHROUGH
ON SKIS III
THE NEW SKIS

**HOW TO GET THE BEST
PERFORMANCE FROM
YOUR NEW
SHAPED
SKIS**

**THIRD IN A SERIES OF
VIDEO SKI LESSONS
WITH LITO**

Short, shaped (or deep-sidecut) skis were nothing short of a revolution when they first appeared. The revolution continues. But so does the question of how to get the most out of these amazing skis. Yes, they do make everything easier. Great turns are easier, but so are lousy turns. And we want the former. In this hour-long DVD, the third in the Breakthrough on Skis video series, Lito shows you how to use these great new skiing tools to best effect. A revelation!

"Most revealing are the close-ups of the demonstrators' skis, designed to give the viewer a "fresh view of what really happens down at the snow level, where skier meets the mountain."

Skiing Magazine

Not technique this time, but a book length celebration of the pure joy of life on skis. This collection of Lito's best essays, stories and poems about skiing is richly illustrated with dramatic color photos of skiing around the world—the work of Lito's wife and partner, photographer Linde Waidhofer. Lito and Linde have collaborated on other book projects too, about wild landscapes of the American West and Chile's Patagonia. This hardback book is available through *www.BreakthroughOnSkis.com*. Other photo books by Linde Waidhofer as well as portfolios of her landscape images from North America and also Patagonia are available on Linde's web site, *www.WesternEye.com*.

Made in the USA
San Bernardino, CA
24 January 2016